SFX LIBRARY

0002

G000164495

A GUIDE

ate shown below

Antony and Cleopatra

MARY HARTLEY

WITH TONY BUZAN

Hodder & Stoughton

THE LIBRARY
SAINT FRANCIS XAVIER
SIXTH FORM COLLEGE
MALWOOD ROAD, SW12 8EN

SAINT FRANCIS XAVIER
SIXTH FORM COLLEGE
MALWOOD ROAD SW12 8EN

1/8/03 LIBRARY 3.99

29544 / 822.33 ANT SHA

ISBN 0 340 80300 2

First published 2001
Impression number   10 9 8 7 6 5 4 3 2 1
Year   2006 2005 2004 2003 2002 2001

The 'Teach Yourself' name and logo are registered trade marks of
Hodder & Stoughton Ltd.

Copyright © 2001 Mary Hartley
Introduction ('Revision for A-level literature success') copyright © 2001 Tony Buzan

All rights reserved. No part of this publication may be reproduced or transmitted in
any form or by any means, electronic or mechanical, including photocopy, recording,
or any information storage and retrieval system, without permission in writing from
the publisher or under licence from the Copyright Licensing Agency Limited.
Further details of such licences (for reprographic reproduction) may be obtained
from the Copyright Licensing Agency Limited, of 90 Tottenham Court Road,
London W1P 9HE.

Cover photograph: Donald Cooper, Photostage
Illustrations: David Ashby
Mind Maps: Kate Boyd

Typeset by Transet Limited, Coventry, England.
Printed in Great Britain for Hodder & Stoughton Educational, a division of
Hodder Headline Plc, 338 Euston Road, London NW1 3BH by Cox and Wyman Ltd,
Reading, Berks.

CONTENTS

You are now in the most important educational stage of your life, and are soon to take English Literature exams that may have a major impact on your future career and goals. As one A-level student put it: 'It's crunch time!'

At this crucial stage of your life the one thing you need even more than subject knowledge is the knowledge of *how* to remember, *how* to read faster, *how* to comprehend, *how* to study, *how* to take notes and *how* to organize your thoughts. You need to know how to *think*; you need a basic introduction on how to use that super bio-computer inside your head – your brain.

The next eight pages contain a goldmine of information on how you can achieve success both at school and in your A-level English Literature exams, as well as in your professional or university career. These eight pages will give you skills that will enable you to be successful in *all* your academic pursuits. You will learn:

◆ How to recall more *while* you are learning.
◆ How to recall more *after* you have finished a class or a study period.
◆ How to use special techniques to improve your memory.
◆ How to use a revolutionary note-taking technique called Mind Maps that will double your memory and help you to write essays and answer exam questions.
◆ How to read everything faster while at the same time improving your comprehension and concentration.
◆ How to zap your revision!

How to understand, improve and master your memory of Literature Guides

Your memory really is like a muscle. Don't exercise it and it will grow weaker; *do* exercise it properly and it will grow incredibly more powerful. There are really only four main things you need to understand about your memory in order to increase its power dramatically:

Recall during learning
– YOU MUST TAKE BREAKS!

When you are studying, your memory can concentrate, understand and recall well for between 20 and 45 minutes at a time. Then it *needs* a break. If you carry on for longer than this without one, your memory starts to break down. If you study for hours non-stop, you will remember only a fraction of what you have been trying to learn, and you will have wasted valuable revision time.

So, ideally, *study for less than an hour*, then take a five- to ten-minute break. During this break listen to music, go for a walk, do some exercise, or just daydream. (Daydreaming is a necessary brain-power booster – geniuses do it regularly.) During the break your brain will be sorting out what it has been learning and you will go back to your study with the new information safely stored and organized in your memory banks. Make *sure* you take breaks at regular intervals as you work through the *Literature Guides*.

Recall after learning
– SURFING THE WAVES OF YOUR MEMORY

What do you think begins to happen to your memory straight *after* you have finished learning something? Does it immediately start forgetting? No! Surprisingly, your brain actually *increases* its power and carries on remembering. For a short time after your study session, your brain integrates the information, making a more complete picture of everything it has just learnt. Only then does the rapid decline in memory begin, as much as 80 per cent of what you have learnt can be forgotten in a day.

However, if you catch the top of the wave of your memory, and briefly review what you have been revising at the correct time, the memory is stamped in far more strongly, and stays at the crest of the wave for a much longer time. To maximize your brain's power to remember, take a few minutes and use a Mind Map to review what you have learnt at the end of a day. Then review it at the end of a week, again at the end of a month, and finally a week before the exams. That way you'll surf-ride your memory wave all the way to your exam, success and beyond!

The memory principle of association

The muscle of your memory becomes stronger when it can **associate** – when it can link things together.

Think about your best friend, and all the things your mind *automatically* links with that person. Think about your favourite hobby, and all the associations your mind has when you think about (remember!) that hobby.

When you are studying, use this memory principle to make associations between the elements in your subjects, and thus to improve both your memory and your chances of success.

The memory principle of imagination

The muscle of your memory will improve significantly if you can produce big images in your mind. Rather than just memorizing the name of a character, imagine that character of the novel or play as if you were a video producer filming that person's life. The same goes for images in poetry.

In *all* your subjects use the **imagination** memory principle.

Throughout this *Literature Guide* you will find special association and imagination techniques (called mnemonics after the Greek goddess Mnemosyne) that will make it much easier for you to remember the topic being discussed. Look out for them!

Your new success formula: Mind Maps®

You have noticed that when people go on holidays, or travel, they take maps. Why? To give them a general picture of where they are going, to help them locate places of special interest and importance, to help them find things more easily, and to help them remember distances and locations, etc.

It is exactly the same with your mind and with study. If you have a 'map of the territory' of what you have to learn, then everything is easier. In learning and study, the Mind Map is that special tool.

As well as helping you with all areas of study, the Mind Map actually *mirrors the way your brain works.* Your Mind Maps can be used for taking notes from your study books, for taking notes in class, for preparing your homework, for presenting your homework, for reviewing your tests, for checking your and your friends' knowledge in any subject, and for *helping you understand anything you learn.* Mind Maps are especially useful in English literature, as they allow you to map out the whole territory of a novel, play or poem, giving you an 'at-a-glance' snapshot of all the key information you need to know.

The Mind Maps in the *Literature Guide* use, throughout, **imagination** and **association**. As such, they automatically strengthen your memory muscle every time you use them. Throughout this guide you will find Mind Maps that summarize the most important areas of the English Literature guide you are studying. Study these Mind Maps, add some colour, personalize them, and then have a go at making your own Mind Maps of the work you are studying – you will remember them far better! Put them on your walls and in your files for a quick and easy review. Mind Maps are fast, efficient, effective and, importantly, *fun* to do!

HOW TO DRAW A MIND MAP

1 Start in the middle of the page with the page turned sideways. This gives your brain more radiant freedom for its thoughts.

2 Always start by drawing a picture or symbol of the novel or its title. Why? Because *a picture is worth a thousand words to your brain.* Try to use at least three colours, as colour helps your memory even more.

3 Let your thoughts flow, and write or draw your ideas on coloured branching lines connected to your central image. The key symbols and words are the headings for your topic.

4 Next, add facts and ideas by drawing more, smaller, branches on to the appropriate main branches, just like a tree.

5 Always print your word clearly on its line. Use only one word per line.

6 To link ideas and thoughts on different branches, use arrows, colours, underlining and boxes.

HOW TO READ A MIND MAP

1 Begin in the centre, the focus of your novel, play or poem.

2 The words/images attached to the centre are like chapter headings; read them next.

3 Always read out from the centre, in every direction (even on the left-hand side, where you will read from right to left, instead of the usual left to right).

USING MIND MAPS

Mind Maps are a versatile tool – use them for taking notes in class or from books, for solving problems, for brainstorming with friends, and for reviewing and revising for exams – their uses are infinite! You will find them invaluable for planning essays for coursework and exams. Number your main branches in the order in which you want to use them and off you go – the main headings for your essay are done and all your ideas are logically organized!

Super speed reading and study

What do you think happens to your comprehension as your reading speed rises? 'It goes down!' Wrong! It seems incredible, but it has been proved – the faster you read, the more you comprehend and remember!

So here are some tips to help you to practise reading faster – you'll cover the ground much more quickly, remember more, *and* have more time for revision and leisure activities!

SUPER SPEED READING

1 First read the whole text (whether it's a lengthy book or an exam paper) very quickly, to give your brain an overall idea of what's ahead and get it working.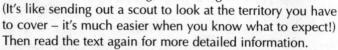
(It's like sending out a scout to look at the territory you have to cover – it's much easier when you know what to expect!) Then read the text again for more detailed information.
2 Have the text a reasonable distance away from your eyes. In this way your eye/brain system will be able to see more at a glance, and will naturally begin to read faster.
3 Take in groups of words at a time. Rather than reading 'slowly and carefully' read faster, more enthusiastically. Your comprehension will rocket!
4 Take in phrases rather than single words while you read.
5 Use a guide. Your eyes are designed to follow movement, so a thin pencil underneath the lines you are reading, moved smoothly along, will 'pull' your eyes to faster speeds.

HOW TO MAKE STUDY EASY FOR YOUR BRAIN

When you are going somewhere, is it easier to know beforehand where you are going, or not? Obviously it is easier if you *do* know. It is the same for your brain and a book. When you get a new book, there are seven things you can do to help your brain get to 'know the territory' faster:

1 Scan through the whole book in less than 20 minutes, as you would do if you were in a shop thinking whether or not to buy it. This gives your brain *control*.

2 Think about what you already know about the subject. You'll often find out it's a lot more than you thought. A good way of doing this is to do a quick Mind Map on *everything you know* after you have skimmed through it.

3 Ask who, what, why, where, when and how questions about what is in the book. Questions help your brain 'fish' the knowledge out.

4 Ask your friends what they know about the subject. This helps them review the knowledge in their own brains, and helps your brain get new knowledge about what you are studying.

5 Have another quick speed read through the book, this time looking for any diagrams, pictures and illustrations, and also at the beginnings and ends of chapters. Most information is contained in the beginnings and ends.

6 If you come across any difficult parts in your book, mark them and *move on*. Your brain *will* be able to solve the problems when you come back to them a bit later. Much like saving the difficult bits of a jigsaw puzzle for later. When you have finished the book, quickly review it one more time and then discuss it with friends. This will lodge it permanently in your memory banks.

7 Build up a Mind Map as you study the book. This helps your brain to organize and hold (remember!) information as you study.

Helpful hints for exam revision

◆ To avoid **exam panic** cram at the *start* of your course, not the end. It takes the same amount of time, so you may as well use it where it is best placed!

◆ Use Mind Maps throughout your course, and build a Master Mind Map for each subject – a giant Mind Map that summarizes everything you know about the subject.

◆ Use memory techniques such as mnemonics (verses or systems for remembering things like dates and events or lists).

◆ Get together with one or two friends to revise, compare Mind Maps, and discuss topics.

AND FINALLY ...

◆ *Have fun while you learn* – studies show that those people who enjoy what they are doing understand and remember it more, and generally do better.

◆ *Use your teachers* as resource centres. Ask them for help with specific topics and with more general advice on how you can improve your all-round performance.

◆ *Personalize your **Literature Revision Guide*** by underlining and highlighting, by adding notes and pictures. Allow your brain to have a conversation with it!

Your amazing brain and its amazing cells

Your brain is like a super, *super*, SUPER computer. The world's best computers have only a few thousand or hundred thousand computer chips. Your brain has 'computer chips' too, and they are called brain cells. Unlike the computer, you do not have only a few thousand computer chips – the number of brain cells in your head is a *million MILLION*!! This means you are a genius just waiting to discover yourself! All you have to do is learn how to get those brain cells working together, and you'll not only become more smart, you'll have more free time to pursue your other fun activities.

The more you understand your amazing brain the more it will repay and amaze you!

Apply its power to this *Literature Guide*!

(Tony Buzan)

HOW TO USE THIS GUIDE

This guide assumes that you have already read *Antony and Cleopatra*, although you could read 'Context' and 'The story of *Antony and Cleopatra*' first. It is best to use the guide alongside the play. You could read the 'Characterization' and 'Themes' sections without referring to it, but you will get more out of these if you do.

The sections

The 'Commentary' section can be used in a number of ways. One way is to read a scene of the play, and then read the relevant commentary. Keep on until you come to a test section, test yourself – then have a break! Alternatively, read the Commentary for a scene, then read that scene in the play, then go back to the Commentary. See what works best for you.

'Critical approaches' sums up the main critical views and interpretations of the play. Your own response is important, but be aware of these approaches too.

'How to get an "A" in English Literature' gives valuable advice on what to look for in a text, and what skills you need to develop in order to achieve your personal best.

'The exam essay' is a useful 'night before' reminder of how to tackle exam questions, though it will help you more if you also look at it much earlier in the year. 'Model answer' gives an example A-grade essay and the Mind Map and plan used to write it.

The questions

Whenever you come across a question in the guide with a star ✪ in front of it, think about it for a moment. You could make a Mini Mind Map or a few notes to focus your mind. There is not usually a 'right' answer to these: it is important for you to develop your own opinions if you want to get an 'A'. The

'Test' sections are designed to take you about 15–20 minutes each – time well spent. Take a short break after each one.

Key to icons

A **theme** is an idea explored by an author. Whenever a theme is dealt with in the guide, the appropriate icon is used. This means you can find where a theme is mentioned by flicking through the book. Go on – try it now!

Love and
sexuality

Judgement

Duty and order

Power

LANGUAGE, STYLE AND STRUCTURE

This heading and icon are used in the Commentary wherever there is a special section on the author's choice of words and imagery and the overall plot structure.

Historical context

Although William Shakespeare is generally referred to as an Elizabethan writer, two monarchs ruled during his life, Elizabeth I (1533–1603) and James I (1566–1625). *Antony and Cleopatra* was probably written in 1607, so will have been performed during the reign of James. (See 'Critical approaches' for the relationship between the play and the court of King James.) Under Elizabeth I England enjoyed a period of prosperity. The defeat of the Spanish Armada in 1588 led to a growth in the self-confidence of the nation, and the middle classes were able to grow and prosper, but towards the end of Elizabeth's reign the national mood was far less optimistic. James I brought new hope for the future, but by the time that *Antony and Cleopatra* was written there was some disillusion with his reign, and people were beginning to think nostalgically of the so-called 'golden age' under Elizabeth's rule. It is likely that Shakespeare's audience would have made connections between Elizabeth I and the presentation of Cleopatra. Descriptions of the behaviour of Elizabeth include accounts of her proud and imperious nature and her capricious exhibitions of tempestuous anger followed by displays of affection. Elizabeth was also said to combine art and nature. ✪ Find examples in the text where these qualities are seen in Cleopatra.

The Elizabethan world

EXPLORATION

Concepts of the world were changing during the sixteenth and seventeenth centuries. The voyage of Christopher Columbus to America in 1492 had opened people's eyes to the vastness and strangeness of the world, and sailors such as Sir Francis Drake (1545–96) and Sir Walter Raleigh (1552–1618) kept alive a sense of the possibilities of the world, bringing back stories of different peoples and customs. Elizabeth I sponsored some voyages of exploration, and trading companies were set up to discover new lands and new areas to be plundered.

SCIENCE

Scientific ideas were challenged by the scholars of the Renaissance. Galileo (1564–1642) revealed that the Sun is the centre of the planetary system, challenging the old idea that the Earth was the centre of the universe. However, the idea persisted that the universe consisted of nine spheres, with God inhabiting the outermost, and the Moon and the Earth the innermost. ✪ Look for references to the spheres as you read *Antony and Cleopatra*. Another belief that is reflected in many of Shakespeare's plays, including *Antony and Cleopatra*, was that the stars influenced people and events. ✪ How far do the characters in *Antony and Cleopatra* feel in control of their own destiny, and how far do they feel that their fate is predetermined?

RELIGION

The split between England and the Roman Catholic Church had far-reaching effects on the state and the monarchy. The State Church arose in the first place from Henry VIII's break with the Church of Rome, when Henry declared himself to be Supreme Head of the English Church. Under Mary Tudor, however, attempts were made to return England to the Roman Catholic Church. When Mary died, Elizabeth became Queen. She enforced Protestant worship, but with nothing like the zeal with which Mary had promoted the Catholic cause. The breaking away from Rome, known as the Reformation, heralded a period of unrest and challenge to established authority, a mood reflected in many Shakespeare plays.

POLITICS

Elizabeth came to the throne after a period of great upheaval, and her own reign was beset with tensions about an heir to the throne and about the threat from Spain, whose king, Philip II, had been married to Mary Tudor and therefore had a claim to the throne. Elizabeth did not marry, although she had many offers and some favourites, such as the Earl of Essex. Consequently, when she died the nearest claimant was James VI of Scotland. On James's accession to the throne in 1603, England and Scotland were united under one ruler. ✪ James I was seen as the bringer of peace. Who is his equivalent in

Antony and Cleopatra? How are political tensions and power struggles presented in *Antony and Cleopatra*?

The Elizabethan theatre

BUILDINGS AND STRUCTURE

Antony and Cleopatra was written to be produced at the Globe Theatre which was built in 1599. The Elizabethan playhouse was developed from medieval inns and the bear-baiting and bull-baiting arenas of the time. Theatres were three-storeyed buildings surrounding an open-air auditorium, with a stage extending into the middle of the yard and the audience standing or sitting on improvised seats around three sides of it. The stage itself was raised about one and a half metres above ground level, and there was a gallery or balcony behind it. With a diameter of approximately 25 metres, the stage area occupied about half the theatre, which meant that the audience was very near the actors. ❂ How might the proximity of actors and audience affect the construction and content of a play? Think of one or two scenes in *Antony and Cleopatra* which would have benefited from a large stage. Which scenes might make good use of the gallery?

CONVENTIONS AND CONSTRAINTS

There was little or no use of stage scenery, although costumes and props, including items of stage furniture, provided authenticity. ❂ Make a props list for a production of *Antony and Cleopatra*. In which scenes might you want to use (a) a tree, (b) a bed? Because of the lack of scenery, all locations and movements had to be established through the dialogue. Plays were written without act or scene divisions, so movement was swift, without a break. ❂ Which groups of scenes in *Antony and Cleopatra* would gain particular impact from quick transition from one scene to another?

Convention decreed that it was improper for women to appear on the stage, so all female roles were taken by young men. ❂ How does this affect the presentation of Cleopatra and her relationship with Antony?

Literary context

THE RENAISSANCE

The movement known as the Renaissance was a rebirth or renewal of cultural life which began in fourteenth-century Italy. It was characterized by an attitude that challenged old certainties and traditions, and by a revival of interest in classical texts and culture. Some critical attitudes to *Antony and Cleopatra* were shaped by the neo-classical ideas of what a play should be. These ideas stated that drama should conform to the rules of ancient tragedy, with particular reference to the unities of time, place and action, and to the stipulation that comedy and tragedy should not be mixed in the same play. ✪ How far does *Antony and Cleopatra* match these requirements?

Another Renaissance concept which has affected approaches to *Antony and Cleopatra* is the idea of the hero or great man. The idea of heroism is summed up in the quality known as *virtus*, which describes strength and energy. A classical hero would have displayed this quality through his military achievements and his courage in battle; this ideal was modified during the period of the Renaissance to include more courtly attributes of humility and love.

Antony is presented as an old-fashioned hero, whose moral blemishes are excused because of his heroic nature. His preoccupation with honour, his reputation and his ancestry, and his titanic anger, establish Antony as a heroic figure in the eyes of the contemporary audience. At the same time, during the seventeenth century, changes in the concept of honour were taking place. With the rise of professional armies and changes in the nature of the aristocracy, the old idea of honour gave way to a new code of 'civil' behaviour. Individual success became more important than personal loyalties and chivalrous behaviour. In this context, Antony's sweeping, flamboyant gestures, such as his challenge to single combat and his declarations that he does heroic deeds for the sake of love, may appear outmoded when seen in contrast with the behaviour of Caesar, the representative of the new age.

SOURCES FOR ANTONY AND CLEOPATRA

There are several versions of the story of Antony and Cleopatra with which Shakespeare was probably familiar, and he may also have been influenced by the epic poem *The Aeneid*, written by the Roman poet Virgil about thirteen years after the battle of Actium (31 BCE). The poem's hero, Aeneas, puts his duty as a Roman above his love for Dido, the queen of Carthage. In *Antony and Cleopatra*, the dying Antony refers to Dido and Aeneas as he imagines himself and Cleopatra taking over their roles as chief lovers in the Underworld.

The major source for this and other Shakespeare plays is Sir Thomas North's translation of Plutarch's *Lives of the Greeks and Romans*. Plutarch was a Greek who wrote in the first century CE, not long after the events he describes. His accounts show his interest in human behaviour and motivation, and demonstrate his awareness of the mixture of good and bad in all human beings. This approach is reflected in Shakespeare's plays, particularly in *Antony and Cleopatra*. Shakespeare uses details and even phrases from North's translation, but makes many changes to the original source, selecting and adapting material for his own purposes.

Try this

? In each of the following examples, say how Shakespeare altered the original source material. For each one, decide what the alteration reveals about Shakespeare's purpose.

In Plutarch's account:

1 Antony lived with Octavia for a number of years, and they had several children.
2 Bacchus, the god of wine, abandoned Antony after the battle near Alexandria.
3 Very little is said about Enobarbus.
4 Antony was shown to be cruel and tyrannical, and dealt in bribery and extortion.
5 Scarus defected to Caesar.
6 Antony ordered Pompey to be killed.
7 Cleopatra opposed Antony's sending Enobarbus's treasure after him.
8 Octavius Caesar enjoyed sports and fishing.

Historical background to Antony and Cleopatra

In 60 BCE Julius Caesar, Pompey the Great (father of the Pompey in *Antony and Cleopatra*) and Marcus Crassus formed the first triumvirate (rule by three) and jointly controlled the Roman Empire. ❂ How does Pompey the Great feature in *Antony and Cleopatra*? Caesar and Pompey clashed, and Caesar went to Egypt and began his affair with Cleopatra. ❂ How is this affair referred to in *Antony and Cleopatra*? Cleopatra herself was in conflict with her brother Ptolemy, whose supporters killed Pompey. Following this, Caesar became virtually the sole ruler, and was seen by some Republican Romans to be taking on the status of a king, an idea that was anathema to Roman ideas of freedom and citizenship. A group of senators, led by Brutus and Cassius, assassinated Caesar. Mark Antony, together with Caesar's great-nephew Octavius, and a rich nobleman, Lepidus, fought Caesar's killers, defeating Brutus and Cassius at Philippi. ❂ In *Antony and Cleopatra*, what aspect of Antony's behaviour at Philippi is described? What aspect of Octavius's behaviour is described?

Antony, Caesar and Lepidus became the second triumvirate. Antony travelled east on an expedition against the Parthians, and on his way arranged a meeting with Cleopatra to ask her to account for her support of Cassius following the murder of Caesar. They met on the River Cydnus, and the rest is history ...

Julius Caesar

Antony and Cleopatra may be seen as a kind of sequel to *Julius Caesar*, written around 1599. The earlier play describes the events surrounding the murder of Julius Caesar in 44 BCE, and introduces Antony and Octavius, as well as other characters who are referred to in *Antony and Cleopatra*. It ends with the deaths of Brutus and Cassius at Philippi in 42 BCE; *Antony and Cleopatra* begins in 40 BCE with Antony, Octavius and Lepidus established as the new triumvirate.

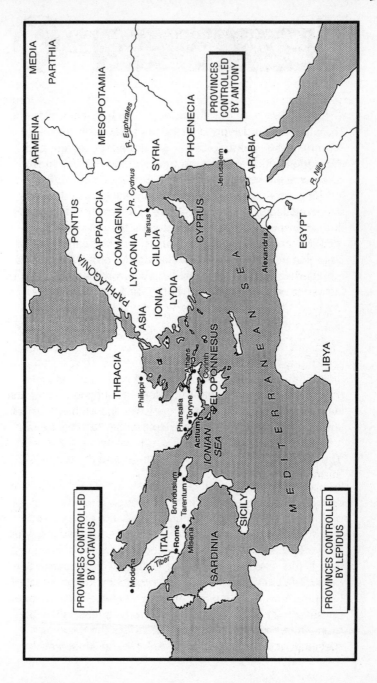

PROVINCES CONTROLLED BY ANTONY

PROVINCES CONTROLLED BY OCTAVIUS

PROVINCES CONTROLLED BY LEPIDUS

MEDIA
PARTHIA
ARMENIA
MESOPOTAMIA
R. Euphrates
PONTUS
CAPPADOCIA
COMAGENIA
PAPHLAGONIA
LYCAONIA
R. Cydnus
SYRIA
PHOENECIA
Tarsus
CILICIA
Jerusalem
ARABIA
ASIA
IONIA
LYDIA
CYPRUS
R. Nile
EGYPT
Alexandria
MEDITERRANEAN SEA
THRACIA
Philippi
Athens
Corinth
PELOPONNESUS
Pharsalia
Toryne
Actium
IONIAN SEA
LIBYA
Brundusium
Tarentum
ITALY
Rome
Misena
R. Tiber
SARDINIA
SICILY
Modena

Act 1

The play starts in Egypt, in Cleopatra's palace in Alexandria. Antony's soldiers disapprove of what they see as Antony's infatuation with Cleopatra. Antony ignores Caesar's messenger, and asserts his love for Cleopatra. As a soothsayer tells fortunes at Cleopatra's court, Antony finally listens to the messengers, much to Cleopatra's dismay. There is internal conflict in the Roman Empire: Pompey is threatening the power of Caesar; the Parthian force under Labienus is invading part of the Empire; and Antony's wife Fulvia and her brother Lucius have mounted an unsuccessful rebellion against Caesar in Italy. The last piece of news is that Fulvia has died.

Antony resolves to leave for Rome, and tells Enobarbus his decision. Enobarbus anticipates passionate opposition from Cleopatra, and indeed she does try a succession of tactics to get Antony to stay, but to no avail. In Rome, Caesar complains bitterly about Antony's behaviour and neglect of duty. He hopes that Antony will return to Rome to support Caesar and Lepidus in the fight against Pompey. Cleopatra misses Antony, and in his absence reveals the depth of her feelings for him.

Act 2

Pompey assesses his position, made stronger by the personal conflicts among the triumvirate. However, news that Antony is on his way to Rome makes Pompey fear the power of a reunited opposition. At an uneasy meeting in Lepidus's house, Caesar and Antony engage in accusations and explanations, with Lepidus keeping the peace, until they finally agree to reconcile their differences in order to deal with the threat of Pompey. Agrippa proposes a marriage between Antony and Caesar's sister Octavia, to which Antony agrees. When the triumvirate have left, Enobarbus describes the dazzling spectacle of the first meeting of Antony and Cleopatra.

The soothsayer reveals to Antony that Caesar will always outshine him, and Antony decides to return to Egypt where his heart lies, in spite of the marriage he has just contracted. Meanwhile, in Egypt, Cleopatra hears of Antony's marriage. In anger and jealousy, she beats the poor messenger who brings the news.

The triumvirs and Pompey meet and agree a peace treaty. Enobarbus and Menas reveal the cracks beneath the surface of amity. Menas feels that Pompey should not agree to the disadvantageous terms offered, and Enobarbus doubts that the alliance between Caesar and Antony will last. The treaty is celebrated at a feast on board Pompey's galley, from which Lepidus is carried off drunk. Menas suggests to Pompey that he should cut the throats of Antony, Caesar and Lepidus while he has the chance. Pompey refuses to condone this idea, although he would have applauded its being done without his knowledge.

Act 3

Ventidius has triumphed over the Parthians, but is reluctant to appear too successful in battle. Antony and Octavia take their leave of Caesar, who warns Antony to take care of her. In Egypt, Cleopatra questions the messenger about Octavia's appearance. Antony complains to Octavia that Caesar has broken the treaty with Pompey and has spoken disparagingly of him. Octavia asks to go to Rome to mediate between Caesar and Antony. Eros reports that Caesar has had Lepidus imprisoned, and that one of Antony's officers has murdered Pompey. Caesar complains to his followers that Antony has held a public ceremony at which Cleopatra was enthroned and endowed with kingdoms. Octavia's unexpected, low-key arrival further angers Caesar.

The action shifts to the scene of war at Actium. Cleopatra angers Enobarbus by insisting on being present in Antony's camp. Antony ignores the advice of his army to fight by land, and engages in a sea battle, encouraged by Cleopatra. As Caesar and Antony await the outcome of the battle at sea, Enobarbus describes how Cleopatra, for no apparent reason, turned sail and fled from the fight. She was followed by

Antony. Canidius decides to defect to Caesar, but Enobarbus, against his better judgement, stays with Antony.

After the battle Antony is deeply ashamed. He blames Cleopatra for his loss of honour, but then forgives her. Antony sends his ambassador to Caesar. Caesar refuses Antony's requests, and sends Thidias to try to win Cleopatra from Antony. Antony challenges Caesar to single combat. Enobarbus sees that Antony's judgement is failing, and questions the wisdom of his own decision to stay with his master.

Thidias makes his approaches to the Queen on Caesar's behalf. Antony finds Thidias kissing her hand, and in a rage has Thidias whipped. He accuses Cleopatra of betraying him, but she convinces him of her love. Antony prepares to fight Caesar again, and calls for one more night of revelry. Enobarbus plans to leave him.

Act 4

Caesar rejects Antony's challenge to a sword fight. Antony calls his servants together and thanks them for their loyal service, as if addressing them for the last time, but then claims to be ready for victory the next day. The guards hear ominous music in the air and under the earth. Eros and Cleopatra help to arm Antony for battle. Before the fight, Antony hears that Enobarbus has deserted, despite which he orders that Enobarbus's treasure should be sent after him. This gesture fills Enobarbus with guilt and remorse and he decides not to fight, but to die.

Antony's soldiers force Caesar's army to retreat. Antony leads his troops triumphantly through Alexandria, and presents Scarus for Cleopatra's praise and reward. In Caesar's camp, Enobarbus dies of grief.

At the final battle, the Egyptian fleet suddenly surrenders. Antony denounces Cleopatra's betrayal and vows to kill her. Cleopatra locks herself in her monument and sends word to Antony that she has killed herself. When Antony receives the false report of Cleopatra's death, he vows to take his own life. He asks Eros to kill him, but Eros kills himself rather than perform such an act. Antony falls on his own sword but does not inflict an immediately fatal wound. When the news arrives that Cleopatra is in fact alive, he asks to be taken to her. At the monument, Antony dies in Cleopatra's arms.

Act 5

Caesar receives the news of Antony's death. Intending to keep Cleopatra alive to display in his triumphant procession, Caesar sends Proculeius to reassure her of his good intentions and to prevent her from committing suicide. As Proculeius talks to Cleopatra, Caesar's soldiers break in and Cleopatra tries to stab herself. Dolabella tells Cleopatra what Caesar's real intentions are. Caesar visits Cleopatra and promises that she will not be harmed, but if she kills herself her children will be put to death. Cleopatra hands Caesar what she claims is a full inventory of her treasure, but her treasurer Seleucus reveals that she has kept some back. Caesar approves of this action, and allows her to keep all her assets.

Cleopatra makes arrangements to die. She has already found out painless and non-disfiguring ways to die, and has organized a countryman to smuggle in poisonous snakes, concealed in a basket of figs. She asks her maids to dress her in her crown and her royal regalia. She kisses her servants farewell, and Iras falls down dead. Cleopatra applies an asp to her breast, and dies with Antony's name on her lips. Charmian takes an asp for herself, and dies as she adjusts Cleopatra's crown. Caesar enters and discovers that he has been foiled. He pays tribute to Cleopatra, and orders that she and Antony should be buried together.

The Mini Mind Map above summarizes the main characters in *Antony and Cleopatra*. When you have read this section, look at the full Mind Map on p. 22, then make a copy of the Mini Mind Map and try to add to it from memory.

Antony and Cleopatra is dominated by the two main characters, whose complex and sometimes puzzling personalities encapsulate the play's ambiguous nature. Other characters, too, are not easily judged, and invite responses that can be contradictory and not clear-cut.

Mark Antony

Antony is the central figure of the play, with the largest part. Although he dies at the end of Act 4, his presence dominates the fifth act as his spirit is constantly evoked through Cleopatra's words and actions.

Shakespeare adapted the presentation of Antony in Plutarch's account in order to create a sympathetic tragic hero. Although Antony's faults and frailties are apparent, his nobility and greatness make him tower above others and maintain his status as a mythic figure. Maecenas says his *taints and honours waged equal with him* (Act 5, scene 1, lines 30–1). ❂ Some readers believe that his honour in fact outweighs his faults. What do you think?

12

It is an aspect of the play's complex nature that Antony's flaws in some cases may be seen as his strengths. The Roman view of Antony is that he has become a *strumpet's fool* (Act 1, scene 1, line 13) and *the bellows and the fan/ To cool a gypsy's lust* (Act 1, scene 1, lines 9–10). His infatuation for Cleopatra causes him to neglect his political and military duties, make disastrous decisions and let down his closest friends and admirers. However, what the Romans see as *the itch of his affection* (Act 3, scene 13, line 7) is seen very differently by Antony. He places a value on his love for Cleopatra which goes beyond earthly boundaries and creates a nobility which can only be expressed in cosmic terms. Antony sees this emotional experience as liberating and life-enhancing – *The nobleness of life/ Is to do thus* (Act 1, scene 1, lines 38–9) – while others see him as chained and ultimately destroyed by it. You may think that the emotional impact and direction of the play supports the idea that passionate intense experience is of more value than duty and correctness; on the other hand, you may think that Antony is in the end a *noble ruin* (Act 3, scene 10, line 19) who loses his moral sense.

Many of Antony's actions do demonstrate the lack of morality and self-control of which he is accused. In some instances, Antony's honest acknowledgement of his faults increases our respect for him, as when he admits that *poisoned hours* (Act 1, scene 2, line 98) caused him to forget himself and lose his sense of duty. Behaviour such as his shameful treatment of Octavia and Thidias, and his lack of good judgement and self-discipline in the war against Caesar, is more difficult to place in the context of essential greatness. Sympathy for Antony in spite of these flaws is maintained through a number of devices, including the loyalty of Eros and Enobarbus, both of whom die for love of Antony, and through the appearances of the soothsayer, which suggests that events are inevitable and beyond his control. Another means of gaining sympathy for Antony is the contrast with Caesar, his more successful and far less appealing rival.

Antony's greatness is created through imagery which links him with gods and mythic heroes. He is unique, the *Arabian bird* (Act 3, scene 2, line 12) and the *Jupiter of men* (Act 3, scene 2, line 9). Enobarbus is told *Your emperor/ Continues still a*

Jove (Act 4, scene 6, lines 29–30). The association of Antony with Hercules runs through the play, as do references to his outstanding soldiership: *the greatest soldier of the world* (Act 1, scene 1, line 38); *His soldiership/ Is twice the other twain* (Act 2, scene 2, lines 35–6). The poetic aggrandizement of Antony reaches its height in Cleopatra's vision beginning *His legs bestrid the ocean* (Act 5, scene 2, line 81), a monumental image created after his death, perhaps referring to the Colossus at Rhodes, and one which reverberates beyond the awareness of Antony's faults and mistakes.

Cleopatra

The character of Cleopatra attracts possibly an even wider range of responses than Antony's. Some readers see her as the scheming courtesan who is ultimately responsible for the fall of a great man, while others see her as a magnificent creation with legendary power to allure. To some, she is a complex and paradoxical figure, while others dispute her *infinite variety* (Act 2, scene 1, line 246).

Shakespeare creates Cleopatra through a series of contradictions and paradoxes. Her own self-presentation, bolstered by her followers and maidservants, emphasizes her royalty and power. Antony calls her *your royalty* (Act 1, scene 3, line 92); she is *your highness* (Act 1, scene 5, line 9); Cleopatra reminds the hapless messenger: *Remember/ If e'er thou look'st on majesty* (Act 3, scene 3, lines 17–18). Addresses such as *Royal Egypt! Empress!* (Act 4, scene 15, line 76) constantly remind us of Cleopatra's status. At the same time, she is expressed through her common humanity, as in *a lass unparalleled* (Act 5, scene 2, line 110), *No more but e'en a woman* (Act 4, scene 15, line 78), and the description of her hopping through the public street. Phrases such as *Royal wench!* (Act 2, scene 2, line 235) capture Cleopatra's ability to combine both extremes of personality. Another layer in the construction of Cleopatra is her depiction as sexually threatening and demanding, a Roman interpretation of her character.

Cleopatra is presented through her fluctuating moods and range of behaviours. There is scope for interpreting her behaviour in different ways, as in Act 2, scene 5 when she hears about Antony's marriage. Her treatment of the messenger could stem from her love of Antony and her fear of losing him; at the same time it could indicate a cruel, vicious streak. At other times, such as in Act 1, scene 3, her anger may be genuine or it may be assumed. Cleopatra uses a number of techniques and strategies to keep Antony with her. This could be seen as part of her manipulative nature, but it could also be argued that Cleopatra has every reason to fear Antony's departure. After all, previous lovers have left her and returned to the Roman Empire.

Cleopatra's behaviour at the time of Antony's defeat and death is the source of much speculation. She appears to be flirting and making terms with Caesar's messenger, and the scene with Seleucus reinforces the possibility that she is willing to negotiate with Caesar. Cleopatra's motives for suicide may also be seen as ambiguous. Would she have taken her life if Caesar had offered favourable terms? Some readers maintain that her suicide is less noble than Antony's, but others argue that each of them commits suicide for a number of motives and that no distinction may be drawn between them.

Octavius Caesar

Caesar is presented in an unflattering light overall. His lack of warmth or engaging personal characteristics helps to maintain sympathy for the charismatic Antony. However, Caesar is the successful strategist and ruler, and it could be argued that although he is presented as essentially mediocre, lasting peace would not have been achieved under Antony.

Caesar is a skilled politician who uses and manipulates people for his own ends. He needs Antony's military expertise for the war against Pompey, and in a skilful piece of propaganda, re-creates the mythical Antony who *didst eat strange flesh/ Which some did die to look on* (Act 1, scene 4, lines 67–8) and whose hardships were *born so like a soldier* (Act 1, scene 4, line 71). The Roman people, who do not love Caesar – *Caesar gets money where/ He loses hearts* (Act 2, scene 1, lines 13–14) – will follow the heroic Antony into battle. Caesar clinches the deal by manoeuvring Antony into a marriage with Octavia, then with Antony out of the way in Athens, he breaks the treaty with Pompey and gets rid of Lepidus. His calculating nature may be seen in his measured decision to feast the army and in his strategy of placing Antony's deserters in the front line.

In soldiership, Caesar is inferior to Antony. However, he outstrips his rival in planning and strategy, employing an excellent intelligence service and always being one move ahead. The only person to outwit him is Cleopatra, whose suicide foils his desire to parade her in Rome as an example of his imperial power. In spite of this blow to his plans, at the end of the play Caesar is the victor and the one on whom the *universal peace* (Act 4, scene 6, line 5) depends. His victory is established in political and worldly terms; spiritually and emotionally, Cleopatra and Antony triumph. Some readers claim that Caesar has redeeming features, such as his love for his sister and his admiration of Antony, but his lack of a passionate inner life in a play that celebrates emotional intensity may be seen to indicate his personal inferiority to those he conquers.

Enobarbus

Enobarbus may be seen as the thematic and moral centre of the play. He makes a rational decision to leave Antony, having witnessed his master's disastrous lack of judgement and being certain that defeat is inevitable. However, Enobarbus's emotional reaction to his desertion and Antony's magnanimous response to it causes his death. Through Enobarbus, the qualities of loyalty and love are shown to be more powerful than common sense and reason.

Throughout the play Enobarbus has a role similar to that of a Greek chorus, commenting on and interpreting the action. His remarks prophesy what will happen, as when he says that Antony *will to his Egyptian dish again* (Act 2, scene 6, line 123) and predicts that Antony's marriage to Octavia will cause friction between him and Caesar: *Then shall the sighs of Octavia blow the fire up in Caesar* (Act 2, scene 6, line 124).

When Antony plans his departure, Enobarbus warns him what kind of behaviour to expect from Cleopatra when he tells her that he is leaving. Enobarbus can interpret accurately everything except his own emotional being. (Some readers think that he does misinterpret Cleopatra's behaviour with Thidias. ◑ What do you think?)

Enobarbus carries weight with the audience because he is established as a likeable, trustworthy figure. His blunt speech and witty comments help to present him as the tough, humorous soldier whose honesty and realism earn our respect. His poetic description of Cleopatra's first meeting with Antony is more powerful coming from a character who usually speaks in colloquial prose, and makes us aware that Enobarbus has emotional depth and is capable of imaginative response on several levels.

Lepidus

Lepidus is seen as the weakest of the triumvirate, and becomes something of a figure of fun at the banquet on Pompey's galley and through the mocking comments of Enobarbus and Agrippa. They laugh at the way Lepidus flatters Antony and Caesar – *But he loves Caesar best; yet he loves Antony* (Act 3, scene 2, line 15) – and Enobarbus comments disparagingly *They are his shards, and he their beetle* (Act 3, scene 2, line 21). Lepidus's role as peacemaker between Antony and Caesar shows him to be diplomatic, and his defence of Antony – *I must not think there are/ Evils enough to darken all his goodness* (Act 1, scene 4, lines 10–11) – shows a generous tolerance of Antony's faults. However, these humane qualities are insignificant on the grand scale of events, and our last image of Lepidus is the sight of the third part of the world being carried out drunk. Lepidus's eventual imprisonment serves to illustrate Caesar's ruthlessness.

Octavia

Octavia is presented as a foil to Cleopatra. She is described through images of coldness and lack of emotion – *Octavia is*

17

of a holy, cold and still conversation (Act 2, scene 6, line 120)
– as opposed to Cleopatra's passionate heat. Whereas
Cleopatra rails and emotes, Octavia speaks in a gentle and
unassertive way, as when she whispers in her brother's ear (Act
3, scene 2, line 46). She personifies a Roman ideal of
womanhood, *a piece of virtue* (Act 3, scene 2, line 28) who is
the epitome of *beauty, wisdom, modesty* (Act 2, scene 2, line
251). She is torn between her brother and her husband, and
her internal conflict is expressed through gentle, fragile images
such as the *swansdown feather* (Act 3, scene 2, line 48).
Octavia is sufficiently spirited to act as a mediator between
Caesar and Antony, but we are left with the impression of a
character who has been used by Caesar.

Charmian and Iras

Charmian and Iras are part of the luxurious, pleasurable life of
the Egyptian court. Their earthy comments and jokes about sex
and fertility underline its sensuousness and sexuality. Aspects
of Cleopatra's character are revealed through her relationship
with her maids. Charmian is confident enough to advise
Cleopatra about tactics to keep Antony (Act 1, scene 3) and to
tease her about her previous affairs (Act 1, scene 5), but at the
same time she and Iras are always aware of their mistress's
royalty and her propensity to anger. Their tender care of
Cleopatra at Antony's death and their loving, ritualistic
preparation for Cleopatra's suicide and their own deaths reveal
the depth of their love. As the soothsayer predicts, Charmian
outlives her mistress, if only by a few minutes, and in this way
she contributes to the foreboding undercurrents that run
through the play.

Sextus Pompeius (Pompey)

Pompey is a slight and mediocre figure whose reputation and
power stem from the esteem in which his father Pompey the
Great was held. He seems to be aware that although his
powers are crescent (Act 2, scene 1, line 10) this situation
exists only because the triumvirate are in disarray. In the
meeting with the triumvirates (Act 2, scene 6) he is seen to be

somewhat out of his depth, compensating for his lack of real status by talking a lot and making tactless remarks. He seems to accept the terms he is offered very readily, probably because of Antony's presence. This causes Menas to doubt Pompey's judgement: *The father, Pompey, would ne'er have made this treaty* (Act 2, scene 6, line 84). Pompey's refusal to sanction the murder of the triumvirs, while admitting that he would have welcomed its being done without his knowledge, reveals his sleazy sense of honour. Pompey's response puts Roman honour in an unfavourable light, through which Antony's troubled grappling with the concept reveals him as a more complex and admirable person.

Eros and Canidius

The loyalty of Eros, the servant whom Antony released from slavery, is a moving testimony to Antony. Eros's self-sacrifice in choosing to take his own life rather than kill his master highlights the qualities of affection and fidelity and contrasts them with the self-serving attitude of other characters. Canidius leaves Antony after the defeat at Actium.

Menas and Menacretes

These two are *famous pirates* (Act 1, scene 4, line 49) whose exploits at sea are admired even by their opponents. Enobarbus and Menas praise each other's skills in fighting by land and sea respectively. Menas interprets the political situation accurately, anticipating difficulties in the meeting between Caesar and Antony, and commenting of Antony and Octavia that *the policy of that purpose made more in the marriage than the love of the parties* (Act 2, scene 6, line 117). Menas's disillusion with Pompey's refusal to allow him to murder the triumvirs, and his subsequent desertion, provide a critical comment on the level of personal and political morality in Rome.

Maecenas and Agrippa

Maecenas and Agrippa reveal the Roman fascination with Egypt and Cleopatra. They listen to Enobarbus's accounts with a mixture of envy and disapproval. Agrippa proposes the marriage between Antony and Octavia, possibly or probably on Caesar's instructions. Maecenas and Agrippa respond in shock and horror to Caesar's account of Antony's appearance with Cleopatra in Alexandria (Act 3, scene 6) and are staunch in their support of Caesar. Nevertheless, they pay tribute to Antony on his death.

Proculeius and Dolabella

Antony tells Cleopatra to trust Proculeius, but the latter seems to betray her, as guards burst in as he is negotiating with her. However, Proculeius himself may be surprised by their appearance, in which case his character may demonstrate Caesar's lack of trust in his messenger. Dolabella hears Cleopatra's eulogistic vision of Antony, and informs her of Caesar's intentions, thereby spurring on her plans to commit suicide.

Ventidius and Silius

Antony's officers appear briefly in Act 3, scene 1. Their entry, bearing the dead body of Pacorus, shows the savage reality of military success, and their conversation throws light on their leaders.

Your turn

? Look at the Mini Mind Map at the beginning of this chapter. Develop it with your own ideas. Compare your Mind Map with the one overleaf.

? Draw a pie chart of the major characters. Divide it to show how sympathetic you find each character.

? For each main character, write notes about the kind of actor you would choose for the role. Indicate what physical characteristics you would look for, and the kind of persona each should project.

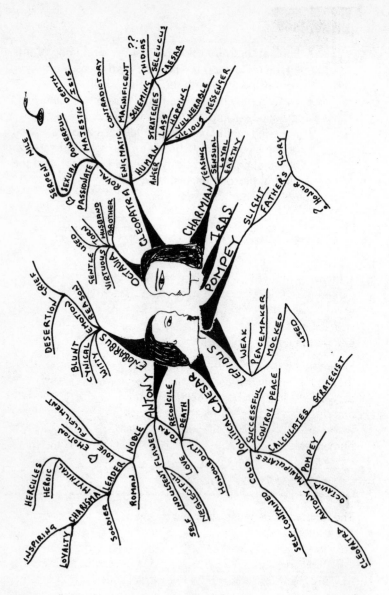

Now you know who's who, take a short break
before focusing on ideas and themes.

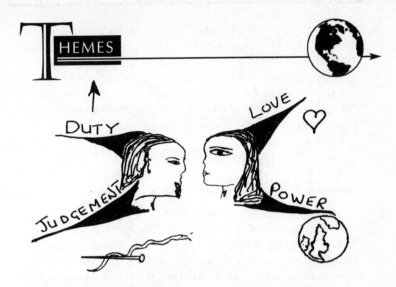

THEMES

A **theme** is an idea that runs through a work and that is explored and developed along the way. The Mini Mind Map above shows the main themes of *Antony and Cleopatra*. Test yourself by copying it and then trying to add to it before comparing your results with the version on p. 27.

The main themes of *Antony and Cleopatra* explore and expand the central conflict in the play, the struggle between the demands of love and self-realization and the demands of duty and discipline. The play raises questions about the nature and worth of worldly power and about the values that define human lives.

Love and sexuality

The love affair between Antony and Cleopatra is the focal point for the exploration of universal themes. The physical and emotional intensity of their love is presented as transcending other considerations and elevating the couple to iconic status. However, their relationship is not always presented in elevated terms. Cleopatra's theatricality and her quicksilver changes of mood and tactics, as she pretends to faint, goads Antony, teases him and rails at him, are sometimes seen as indications of her lack of real feelings for him. In this context, Antony may be seen as helplessly obsessed with a woman who leads him to disaster, a man destroyed by his passion. This passion may be seen as demeaning and ignoble, or glorious and life-enhancing. As in *Romeo and Juliet*, the emotional impetus of the play leads to the final reconciliation of the lovers in death, through which they are transformed to god-like creatures who have raised each other beyond the sphere of petty, worldly emotions.

Duty and order

Throughout the play, ideas of Roman discipline are contrasted with Egyptian laxness and frivolity. Discipline is seen in military terms, Antony's decline being demonstrated by his neglect of his military obligations and his duty to Rome. The Roman disappointment in and censure of Antony is heightened by the contrast between what Antony was and what he is now. The 'old' Antony was no ordinary general, but a hero of Herculean properties who carried the weight of Roman military power and expectations. His abandonment of that role is a blow to his followers on professional and personal levels. Antony's sense of discipline is expressed in his acknowledgement that he must attend to his duties in Rome, and that he must break off from Cleopatra. However, he cannot sustain this commitment without compromising another part of himself. The virtue that he wishes to sustain is his honour, a Roman concept linked to ideas of duty and order, but which in Antony encompasses a wider scope. His suicide may be seen in part as an attempt to reclaim his sense of duty as a Roman and restore his reputation.

Caesar is the embodiment of duty and order, to such an extent that he does not appear to have a private existence. He is successful in the political and military world perhaps for this very reason, because, unlike Antony, his dedication to duty and the pursuit of his aim are not hampered by emotional complications. Caesar's discipline and single-mindedness make him ultimately the unchallenged political winner. However, this is not to say that Roman ideas about duty and order are presented uncritically. At the end of the play Caesar appears as a lesser person than Antony, without his range and depth of emotion and experience in the widest sense. Caesar's own behaviour illustrates the callousness, treachery and ruthlessness that support and maintain Roman order and duty.

Judgement

Through the differences between Rome and Egypt, Shakespeare presents us with conflicting value systems. The reader's judgement and assessment of their rival claims is constantly challenged as each is presented in an ambiguous light.

Egypt offers a world of emotional intensity and sensual enjoyment. This world is judged harshly by the Romans, who are sternly critical of what they see as self-indulgence and lack of discipline. Their condemnation stems from moral self-righteousness, as seen in the words commonly used to describe Cleopatra and the sexual relationship between her and Antony, such as *strumpet, trull, lascivious wassails, fault, filth, vicious.* We are constantly reminded that Antony is married through references such as *thy wife* and *the married woman.* Although the play is set in pagan Rome, the Elizabethan audience would see it in the context of their own Christian morality. ❂ What kind of judgements may be made by a secular audience? To what extent do you think that the play invites moral judgements?

Roman values, however, are also criticized. Rome's ideas of honour and duty are undermined by the duplicity and coldness displayed by representatives of Roman efficiency and success. The Roman view is narrow and restrictive, with no acknowledgement of the life of the imagination. Furthermore, the scenes showing the treaty with Pompey and the banquet on his barge illustrate the lack of integrity that characterizes the Roman pursuit of domination, as the military leaders of the world and their officers are portrayed as thieves, drunkards and hypocrites.

As Roman and Egyptian scenes are swiftly juxtaposed, we are presented with multiple perspectives and conflicting points of view. No definitive judgement is possible. We experience something of the conflict that engages Antony. Judged by entirely Roman or entirely Egyptian standards, he will always fall short. Caught between two irreconcilable opposites, only in death can he be his true self and achieve the *heavenly mingle* (Act 1, scene 5, line 62) that raises him beyond the world of Rome and the world of Egypt.

Power

The grand scale of *Antony and Cleopatra* is created partly through the projection of how much is at stake in the power struggles that take place. Images of the world and the universe not only present the awesome grandeur of the main characters, but also establish the huge scope of the action. Cosmic images of the sun, moon and stars place the drama in a universal context, and a sense of its vastness is further created through references to the land and the sea. References to flies, gnats, snakes, the Nile and crocodiles are reminders of the mystery and power of nature. The all-encompassing sweep of the action is emphasized by the use of place names, which are presented like magnificent rolls of honour to give substance to the kingdoms and provinces for which the characters compete.

The quest for political and military power informs the actions of Antony and Caesar. Cleopatra, too, is motivated by the desire to keep her own position as monarch, and to pass on to her children her title and her kingdoms. Caesar is the most single-minded in his campaign, and his words and actions are governed by his political purposes. Manipulative, ambiguous and pragmatic, he is most suited to worldly power. His final triumph may be seen as an ironic comment on the nature of the world and the power that he wins.

Over to you

> ? Look at the Mini Mind Map at the beginning of this section. Develop it with your own ideas. Compare your finished Mind Map with the one opposite.
> ? Write sentences summarizing the importance of each theme.
> ? Write the keywords of each theme on a large sheet of paper. At random, draw a line between two words. Explain how they are thematically connected.

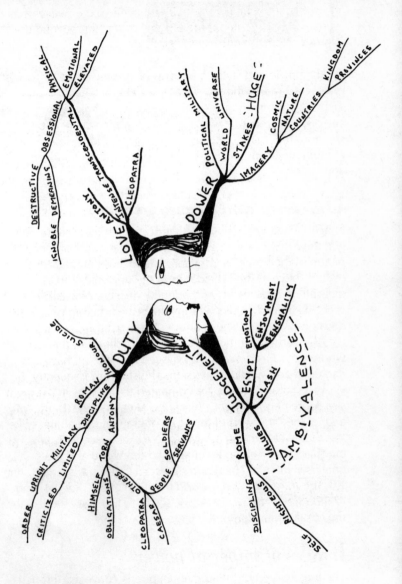

Time for a short break before becoming
linguistic and stylistic.

L ANGUAGE, STYLE AND STRUCTURE

The linguistic and stylistic features of *Antony and Cleopatra* create and reflect the play's complex characterization and themes. Clusters of images, the use of **hyperbole**, **paradox** and **conceit** (see under headings below), supple versification and a structure that makes effective use of pace and juxtaposition combine to shape the reader's response to the characters and action.

Universal and cosmic imagery

Images suggesting universal significance create a sense of the grandeur of Antony and Cleopatra and the transcendental nature of their love. Antony tells Cleopatra that their love extends beyond the boundaries of the universe, and to measure it *Thou needs find out new heaven, new earth* (Act 1, scene 1, line 17). Cleopatra invites heaven to rain poisonous hailstones on her if she is untrue. She herself is associated with Isis, the goddess of the moon, and with Phoebus, the sun god, whose *amorous pinches* (Act 1, scene 5, line 29) have darkened and wrinkled her skin. The stars are frequently evoked. Antony's faults are compared to the stars in the night sky, *More fiery by night's blackness* (Act 1, scene 4, line 13), and, at the other end of the scale of grandeur, Lepidus is like a star that is *called into a huge sphere* (Act 2, scene 7, line 13) but that is ineffective. References to the world and the universe, such as *The world's great snare* (Act 4, scene 9, line 17), the *third part of the world* (Act 2, scene 7, line 84) and *O thou day o' th' world* (Act 4, scene 8, line 13) establish the universal dimension of the play.

Images of imperial power

The huge sweep of the Roman Empire is conveyed through images that suggest power and military conquest. The grandeur of Rome is evoked by Antony's reference to the *wide arch/ Of the ranged empire* (Act 1, scene 1, lines 35–6). Images of arches and pillars, such as *the triple pillar of the world* (Act 1, scene 1, line 12) create a sense of solidity and soaring power. The scope of the Empire is further conveyed through references to provinces and kingdoms. Antony is able *To give a kingdom for a mirth* (Act 1, scene 4, line 18) and Scarus laments that *We have kissed away kingdoms and provinces* (Act 3, scene 10, lines 6–7). Military images, such as Cleopatra's description of Antony as *the arm/ And burgonet of men* (Act 1, scene 5, lines 24–5) and the frequent references to armies and fleets, maintain awareness of the military might of Rome.

Images of fortune

Recurrent images of destiny (the will of the gods) and fortune (chance) encourage the reader to consider how far the characters are in control of their lives, and also add to the interest and suspense of the plot. The role of fate is incorporated in the figure of the soothsayer, whose prophecies all come true. The inevitability of Caesar's success is expressed in images of chance and gambling. The soothsayer tells Antony: *If thou dost play with him at any game,/ Thou art sure to lose* (Act 2, scene 3, lines 25–6), and Antony muses on the truth of this: *The very dice obey him* (Act 2, scene 4, line 33). Antony's decline is expressed in terms of fortune and luck. There was a time when his *hours/ Were nice and lucky* (Act 3, scene 13, lines 183–4), but then his luck deserts him: *Fortune and Antony part here* (Act 4, scene 12, line 19).

Hyperbole

The use of **hyperbole** (an extravagant, exaggerated figure of speech) intensifies the larger-than-life nature of the characters and their emotions. The exalted language of the lovers elevates their passion and places it on a grand scale. Images of Antony as *plated Mars* (Act 1, scene 1, line 4) and the fierce warrior whose heart *hath burst/ The buckles on his breast* (Act 1, scene 1, lines 7–8) are hyperbolic ways of expressing his extraordinary military qualities. Cleopatra's grandiose declaration that she will *unpeople Egypt* (Act 1, scene 5, line 81) is an example of her hyperbolic speech. The association of Cleopatra with the elements, as in *I am fire and air* (Act 5, scene 2, line 283), and her identification with the goddess Isis show how the hyperbolic style presents her in a rarefied light.

The use of **simile** (a comparison using the words 'like' or 'as') and **metaphor** (a figure of speech in which something is spoken of as if it actually is the thing that it resembles) contributes to the hyperbolic effect. Antony the intense lover is said to have become *the bellows and the fan/ To cool a gypsy's lust* (Act 1, scene 1, lines 9–10), and Antony the remarkable soldier leaves for war *like a man of steel* (Act 4, scene 4, line 33). The use of simile contributes to the establishment of Cleopatra as the essence of passion, as in the description of her on the barge in which she is likened to Venus and is surrounded by pretty boys *like smiling Cupids* (Act 2, scene 2, line 212).

Paradox

The use of **paradox** (an apparently contradictory statement) effectively creates Cleopatra's multi-faceted personality. She is exalted beyond the scope of ordinary humanity, yet at the same time she exhibits the common touch. This paradox is presented through the juxtaposition of the hyperbolic description of Cleopatra on the barge, followed by the description of her skipping breathlessly through the public streets. Cleopatra's *infinite variety* (Act 2, scene 3, line 246) is expressed through paradoxes. She *makes hungry/ Where most she satisfies* (Act 2, scene 3, lines 247–8) and can make *defect perfection* (Act 2, scene 3, line 241). Cleopatra is a noble queen and a common harlot, a triumphant lady and a lustful gypsy, a wonderful piece of work and a trull and a strumpet. The paradoxical nature of Cleopatra is also expressed through the use of **oxymoron**, a figure of speech in which contradictory terms are combined, as in *Royal wench!* (Act 2, scene 3, line 237).

Conceit

Another characteristic feature of *Antony and Cleopatra* is the **conceit** (a fanciful, far-fetched comparison, sometimes sustained at length), which is used for both serious and comic effect. An example of the latter is Enobarbus's witty comparison of the gods and the *tailors of the earth* (Act 1, scene 2, lines 158–62), when he consoles Antony on Fulvia's death with the idea that the gods make new people to replace the old, just as tailors make new clothes to replace those which are worn out.

Versification

Shakespeare's verse is usually **blank verse**, that is unrhymed lines in **iambic pentameter**. This means that there are five pairs of syllables in each line, each pair containing an unstressed and a stressed syllable. In *Antony and Cleopatra* Shakespeare adds variety and flexibility with techniques such as **enjambment**, in which the sense and the rhythm run on from line to line. Another technique is variation of the placing of the **caesura**, which is the pause or natural breathing space created by the sense of the words. For example, in *Fulvia thy wife first came into the field* (Act 1, scene 2, line 83), the pause falls after the word 'wife', whereas in *To business that we love we rise betime* (Act 4, scene 4, line 20) the natural pause occurs after the word 'love'.

Occasionally the metre is altered to provide emphasis, as in *Purple the sails, and so perfumed that* (Act 2, scene 2, line 203) where the stress on the first syllable draws attention to the royal colour. In this way, the style of verse reinforces the meaning of the lines. Other ways of varying the verse form include the use of stressed final -ed in verbs and adjectives, and the use of **elision**, where a syllable is left out and words are abridged, as in *I'th'common show-place, where they exercise* (Act 3, scene 6, line 13).

Prose

The dominant form of *Antony and Cleopatra* is poetry, which reflects the exalted level of characters and events, and less than a tenth of the play is in prose. Prose is used (a) by characters of low social status, (b) by those of high social status when in relaxed and informal mode, and (c) for comic effect. Cleopatra's maids and the servants preparing the banquet on Pompey's yacht speak in prose; the comments of the off-duty soldiers Enobarbus, Maecenas and Agrippa are expressed in prose. This is the form used for the conversation on Pompey's galley between the drunken Lepidus and the teasing Antony, and for the conversation of the clown who brings the asps to Cleopatra.

Aspects of character and theme can be conveyed through the shifts from poetry to prose. Enobarbus, for example, speaks in blunt prose in private with Antony, showing their close, confident relationship, but when he comments in prose on the negotiations between the triumvirs, the contrast between his style of speech and the poetic formality of his masters highlights the falseness behind their words. The contrast between Enobarbus's habitual use of prose and his poetic utterances heightens the intensity of the poetry and emphasizes the power of the emotions he is experiencing.

You will find further discussion of language and style throughout the 'Commentary'.

Structure

The structure of the play reflects its central thematic conflict: the rival claims of love and emotional fulfilment, on one hand, and duty, honour and reputation on the other. These conflicting claims, and the split between public and private life, are presented through the structural basis of the play as we constantly shift between Rome and Egypt. Act 1 is set mainly in Egypt, with interruptions from Rome and one scene in Caesar's house. Act 2 shows Antony in his Roman world, with only one Egyptian scene, which shows Cleopatra receiving the news of Antony's marriage. The focal plot point of Act 3 is the battle of Actium. Leading up to this point the action shifts between Alexandria, Athens and Rome, moving to Actium in scene 7.

After this point the focus of the action moves to the conflict between Antony and Caesar, reflected in the large number of very short scenes in each one's camp. Act 4 moves between the two camps and Alexandria, building up to Antony's defeat and suicide in which he finally reconciles within himself Rome and Egypt. The final act is set in Alexandria, briefly in Caesar's camp and then in Cleopatra's monument. The structure of the play and the juxtaposition of scenes reflect the play's thematic concerns.

You're about to enter the worlds of Rome and Egypt — take a break then get into gear!

Act 1 scene 1

Kingdoms and kisses

◆ Roman officers discuss Antony and Cleopatra.
◆ Antony declares his love for Cleopatra.
◆ News arrives from Rome.
◆ Antony refuses to listen to the messenger.

This scene is a dramatic representation of the play as a whole. It begins by presenting a Roman view of the relationship between Antony and Cleopatra, then shows us the two lovers in conversation, ending with a Roman judgement of what we have seen.

Philo's words express the Romans' disapproval of Antony and their disappointment in his unsoldierly behaviour. Antony had been a hero of godlike stature, a military general of mythic proportions, comparable to *plated Mars*, but now his stature is diminished as he expends his energy on satisfying Cleopatra's amorous demands. Contempt for Cleopatra is shown in the references to her tawny front and in the descriptions of her as a gypsy and a strumpet. As the Romans see it, Antony is neglecting his public duty and throwing away his career for a prostitute.

We first see Antony and Cleopatra together as she challenges him to say how much he loves her. Antony's reply, that his love is so great that it exceeds the boundaries of heaven and earth, is reinforced by his dismissal of the news from Rome. Antony's conflict between his duty to Rome and his love of Cleopatra is demonstrated here. Cleopatra, however, does not encourage Antony to disregard Rome; rather, she uses the situation to taunt Antony, suggesting that he is subservient to his wife Fulvia and to Caesar, his younger partner in empire. Her gibes inspire Antony to a passionate and moving declaration that the nobility and grandeur of their love are greater than the mighty Roman Empire. Cleopatra's claims not to believe Antony move him to suggest that they have an evening's entertainment, uninterrupted by *conference harsh*. She knows that she has, for the moment at least, managed to keep Antony's attention focused on her, and that her plea, *Hear the ambassadors*, will be ignored. ✪ What tactics does Cleopatra use to keep Antony interested in her? How certain is she of her power over him?

Philo and Demetrius, representing the Roman point of view, are deeply shocked by Antony's dismissive attitude to Caesar's messenger. Antony is seen as behaving differently from his true self; his distinctive greatness has been lost. ✪ To what extent is the Roman judgement correct? What does it not take into account, or understand? What do you think about Antony's behaviour?

STYLE AND LANGUAGE

The contrast between Rome and Egypt is experienced through the images associated with each place. The uprightness and scope of the Roman Empire are suggested through *the wide arch/ Of the rang'd empire*, and the *triple pillar of the world*. Military references to the *files and musters of the war* suggest the purposeful activity and controlled discipline of Rome. The solidity of Rome is evoked through references to *earth* and *clay*. Egypt, on the other hand, is characterized through images of dissolution, softness, excess and fluidity: Antony's infatuation *o'erflows*; Rome can *melt* into the Tiber; love is enjoyed in *soft hours*.

Antony uses grandiose, sweeping statements to express the transcendental (going beyond usual human experience) nature of his love. His use of **hyperbole** emphasizes the immensity of his passion. Other examples of exaggerated language, such as Antony's heart having *burst/ The buckles on his breast,* and the **simile** which describes Antony's eyes having *glowed like plated Mars*, add to the play's larger-than-life effect, in which emotions and actions are exalted and experienced on a grand scale.

Act 1 scene 2

Fortunes and frivolity

◆ A soothsayer tells the fortunes of Cleopatra's maids.
◆ Antony hears about a series of events from Rome:
  ● The wars fought by his wife and her brother against Caesar.
  ● The death of Antony's wife.
  ● The growing power of Sextus Pompey.
◆ Antony decides to return to Rome.

The atmosphere of Cleopatra's court is conveyed through the playful, bawdy banter between Charmian, Iras and Alexas. Their uninhibited, earthy jesting about adultery, sexuality and fertility illustrates the sensuality associated with Egypt. Charmian teases Alexas, getting back at him for joking that she is likely to be unfaithful to her future husband. She and Iras want the fortune-teller to predict that Alexas marries a woman who cannot have children, and who will make him that Elizabethan figure of fun, a cuckolded (deceived) husband. Charmian's request that she herself should marry rich and powerful men is a light-hearted echo of her mistress's career, just as her mocking prediction for Alexas touches on Antony's fate at the hands of Cleopatra. ✪ Underline all the sexual references in this part of the scene. How do you respond to this aspect of the Egyptian court? What are its positive and its negative qualities?

The soothsayer's riddling predictions, that the fortunes of Charmian and Iras are alike, and that their previous fortune is *fairer* than what is to come, provide an ominous note. The prediction that Charmian will outlive her mistress and her throw-away comment that she loves long life *better than figs* foreshadow the end of the play.

Duty calls

The frivolous mood becomes serious as Roman concerns intervene. Cleopatra is alerted to the change in Antony as a *Roman thought* strikes him. Her sudden refusal to see Antony may indicate her deliberate unpredictability; it may illustrate her deep-rooted fear of losing Antony to his Roman

35

responsibilities. ✪ How do you interpret her behaviour here? Antony's response to the succession of messages from Rome shows him in a different light from the pleasure-loving man of the first scene. He faces up to the truth about the way he and Cleopatra are seen in Rome, and acknowledges his faults. Notice that he uses Philo's derogatory word, *dotage*, to describe his feelings for Cleopatra. The news of Fulvia's death leads him to sober reflection and the decision that he must *from this enchanting Queen break off*.

A plain-speaking friend

Enobarbus is established as Antony's friend and confidant, whose reactions shape our view of Antony and Cleopatra. His response to Antony's decision to leave Egypt is typically shrewd and cynical: he warns Antony to expect a histrionic display from Cleopatra. However, Enobarbus defends Cleopatra when Antony refers to her *cunning*, claiming that her melodramatic behaviour indicates the immensity of her emotions: *We cannot call her winds and waters sighs and tears*. His description of Cleopatra as *a wonderful piece of work* recognizes both her artifice and her attraction. Enobarbus consoles Antony for the loss of his wife with the cynical comment that new wives can be found as easily as new clothes can replace old ones. Antony dismisses as frivolous Enobarbus's final warning that Cleopatra depends on his staying in Egypt. ✪ Why does Antony not want to listen to Enobarbus? How do Enobarbus's comments about Cleopatra affect your view of her? To what extent can you make a definite judgement of her character and behaviour?

Antony's final speech in this scene shows the Roman side of his character. He speaks formally and seriously, assessing the extent of Pompey's threat to Rome. He analyses the political situation, showing understanding of the fickleness of public support and of how Pompey's rise to power has been enabled by the people's adulation of his father. Antony assumes the public role of soldier and general, a role which he has never entirely abandoned. Notice how his choice of pronoun shows his identification with Rome: *our officers*; *Our slippery people*. ✪ What do you think about Antony's decision to return to Rome? How possible is it for him to reconcile the conflicting claims of love and honour?

STYLE AND LANGUAGE

Cleopatra's maids speak in **prose**, the mode of speech often used by lower-status characters in Shakespeare's plays. The use of prose in this section of the scene could be seen as providing relief and a contrast to the play's exalted, intense poetic language, and as being an appropriate form for the women's teasing exchanges. Enobarbus's use of prose in the private discussion with Antony draws attention to their familiar relationship. Prose is also a suitable medium for the bawdy, satirical tone and content of his conversation here, which contains sexual puns such as *when old robes are worn out there are members to make new* (in which *members* can mean materials, and can also refer to the male sexual organs).

Antony's remark *O, then we bring forth weeds,/ When our quick minds lie still, and our ills told us/ Is as our earing* is an example of imagery drawn from ideas about **fertility**, and about the earth. He says that being told our faults uproots them, just as ploughing (*earing*) uproots the weeds from a field. ✪ Find other images of fertility in this scene.

Charmian addresses Isis, the Egyptian **goddess** of the moon, the earth and fertility. In the first speech of the play, Antony is identified with Mars, the **god** of war. Antony is also closely associated with the Greek hero Heracles (Roman form: Hercules), from whom his family was said to descend. ✪ How do these references and associations to gods and goddesses affect the audience's response to the characters and their lives?

Act 1 scene 3

Please don't go

◆ Cleopatra tries to make Antony stay.
◆ Antony leaves for Rome.

Cleopatra is desperate to keep Antony in Egypt. She knows that if he returns to Rome she will lose her hold over him. She uses a range of tactics to keep him interested, first of all sending Alexas to find out what Antony's mood is so that she can behave in the opposite way, and rejecting Charmian's advice that the best way to keep him is to be agreeable and compliant.

The rest of the scene presents the emotional battle between Antony and Cleopatra as she tries to prevent him from leaving. She says that she is sick, and about to faint, then immediately recovers sufficiently to taunt Antony for being under Fulvia's thumb (*What says the married woman? – you may go*) and to accuse him of being unfaithful both to herself and to his wife. With a swift change of tone, she reminds Antony of the intensity of their love:

> *Eternity was in our lips and eyes,*
> *Bliss in our brows' bent; none our parts so poor*
> *But was a race of heaven.*

❂ How does Cleopatra speak these lines? What actions might she perform? Underline the words that express the magnitude of their feelings. What different emotions might Antony experience during the first forty lines of the scene?

Up to this point, Cleopatra dominates the dialogue, with Antony trying in vain to get a word in. Finally, Antony presents his case. He speaks formally, focusing on the political situation that calls him to Rome. At the end of his explanation, he produces what he thinks is his trump card, the news of Fulvia's death. ❂ How might Antony expect Cleopatra to react to this news? Cleopatra seizes the opportunity for another attack on Antony, claiming that his lack of grief for Fulvia's death illustrates how he will react to her own death. Antony, however, does not rise to the bait, and Cleopatra resorts to another fainting fit. She continues to taunt Antony, ironically accusing him of *excellent dissembling*, then moves into teasing mode as she refers to Antony as the *Herculean Roman*, performing the part of an angry man. Finally, Cleopatra has to accept that Antony is determined to leave, and acknowledges that his *honour* requires him to attend to his Roman duties. She manages a dignified farewell, wishing him victory and success.

Try this

? Which of the following words do you associate with
Rome, and which with Egypt? There may be some
qualities that you associate with both. Add your own
words as you go through the play.

> pleasure   emotion   duty   frivolity   admiration
> affection   power   sexuality   politics   loyalty
> betrayal   honour   discipline

? Imagine that you are a Roman soldier or citizen.
Think of three questions that you would like to ask
Antony.

? 'Cleopatra is scheming, self-centred and
manipulative.' What would you say in support of this
statement about Cleopatra? What would you say in
Cleopatra's defence?

? Start two collages, one to represent Rome and one to
represent Egypt. Cut out photos, illustrations and
words from magazines and newspapers and stick
them on to large sheets of paper. You might find it fun
to identify personalities and celebrities who embody
some of the qualities associated with each country.

*Have a short break before meeting Antony's
colleague and rival, Octavius Caesar.*

Act 1 scene 4

'Scarce-bearded Caesar'

◆ Caesar criticizes Antony's behaviour in Egypt.
◆ News arrives that Pompey and his followers are gaining
power at sea.
◆ Caesar hopes that Antony will return to Rome.

Caesar speaks contemptuously of Antony's activities in
Alexandria. Although he claims that his condemnation of

39

Antony is based on political rather than personal grounds, there is an element of personal distaste in Caesar's interpretation of Antony's behaviour. He implies that Antony's pursuit of pleasure is unmanly, and he is offended by Antony's dismissal of his messengers. Caesar says that he disapproves of Antony's pleasure-seeking way of life because of the burden it places on the triumvirate, who have to deal with the difficult current situation without Antony. Antony is like a child who lets the lure of *present pleasure* cloud his judgement. ❂ What do you think of Caesar's attitude? Is he right about Antony?

The language that Caesar uses shows his disgust with Antony's behaviour. Phrases such as *tumble on the bed of Ptolemy*, and the description of Antony mixing with slaves and knaves and reeling drunkenly through the streets in the middle of the day, reveal Caesar's puritanical, rather priggish view and indicate his tendency to take the moral high ground. ❂ What qualities in Antony does his behaviour illustrate? Can you think of positive, non-derogatory ways to describe and illustrate these qualities?

'Leave thy lascivious wassails'

A sense of urgency is created through the succession of messengers bringing the news of Pompey's growing power at sea. Caesar's plea for Antony to return to Rome to give support in the war against Pompey recalls Antony's former greatness. He describes the period after the assassination of Julius Caesar when Antony was driven out of Italy and had to survive famine and hardship. Antony's behaviour on that occasion was honourable and soldierly: he displayed qualities of strength, toughness and endurance. ❂ What does this description add to your view of Antony? What does it add to your impression of Caesar?

The third pillar

Lepidus, the third triumvirate, defends Antony. He says that Antony's faults appear to be worse than they are because they contrast with his general goodness, just as the stars shine out against the night sky. ❂ How does Caesar respond to Lepidus's opinion? At the end of the scene Lepidus asks Caesar to keep him informed of what is going on in the war against Pompey. ❂ How strong a character is Lepidus? How does Caesar seem to treat him?

Act 1 scene 5

When your lover is gone

◆ Cleopatra longs for the absent Antony.
◆ Cleopatra receives news of Antony.
◆ Charmian teases Cleopatra about her former lover, Julius Caesar.

Cleopatra is seen to be in a languid, lethargic mood, wishing to sleep away the period of time that Antony is away. Her joking with the eunuch Mardian about his lack of sexual activity seems to heighten her own longing for Antony, and adds to the Egyptian court's atmosphere of sensuousness and sexuality. Mardian's reference to the sexual relationship between Venus and Mars associates Cleopatra with Venus, the goddess of love, and stirs in Cleopatra an outburst of desire, as in her imagination she evokes a picture of Antony, the great military leader, unrivalled in attack or defence, seated on his horse. This picture combines the erotic – *O happy horse, to bear the weight of Antony!* – and the superhumanly powerful, as she aggrandizes Antony into *The demi-Atlas of this Earth*. In her description, Antony maintains the values of Egypt and of Rome. ❂ Can these values co-exist in reality? Cleopatra's words, like the comments of Philo in the opening scene, elevate Antony to godlike status. ❂ Are people's expectations of Antony realistic? Can he ever live up to his own myth?

Cleopatra recalls Antony's tender description of her as the *serpent of old Nile*. ❂ What ideas do you associate with 'serpent'? Why is it an appropriate term for Cleopatra? Cleopatra reminisces about her former lovers, the powerful leaders Julius Caesar and Gnaeus Pompey, revelling in the awareness of her strong sexual attraction. Even the sun is seen as Cleopatra's lover, its *amorous pinches* making her skin dark and wrinkled. The images of the serpent and the sun emphasize Cleopatra's royal status.

News of Antony

The arrival of Alexas jolts Cleopatra out of her reverie as she eagerly asks for news of Antony. Antony's actions and words, as reported by Alexas, convey a sense of the power and magnificence of the two lovers. Antony promises to add to the gift of the oriental pearl more and more kingdoms to increase the opulence of Cleopatra's throne; his extravagant claims suggest the grandeur of his emotions, and the vast extent of his power. At the same time, the grandiose promises are matched by the picture of the *firm Roman* who *soberly* mounts his horse. Alexas's diplomatic description of Antony's demeanour as *nor sad nor merry* reinforces the idea of Antony poised between Rome and Egypt, combining the roles of military commander and passionate lover.

Alexas chooses his words carefully, not committing himself to a specific report of Antony's appearance. ❂ Why does Alexas have to be diplomatic? What does his approach tell us about Cleopatra? Cleopatra's response to Alexas's description is comical and touching as she spins her own interpretation of it, turning it into an idealized picture of Antony. Cleopatra's response to Charmian's teasing praise of Caesar – *I will give thee bloody teeth* – shows her quick temper and her capacity for violence. ❂ How do you imagine Cleopatra saying these lines? Is she genuinely angry? Is she being playful? Her determination to unpeople Egypt, if necessary, in order to send Antony daily messages, finishes the scene with a flourish as sweeping as Antony's statements, and we are left with an impression of passionate emotions experienced on a grand scale.

STYLE AND LANGUAGE

In Egypt, **food and drink** are associated with pleasure and celebration, seen for example in the cry *Bring in the banquet quickly; wine enough/ Cleopatra's health to drink* (Act 1, scene 2). There is a natural, earthy link between food and sexuality, as when Cleopatra says that she was *a morsel for a monarch*. Cleopatra also uses the image of feeding on *delicious poison* to express the mixture of pain and pleasure she experiences when thinking about the absent Antony. This image is an example of an **oxymoron**, an expression which contains two contradictory ideas. The Roman view of the drinking and feasting associated with Egypt is disapproving. Such behaviour indicates self-indulgence and lack of restraint, qualities which are antipathetic to the Roman ideal.

The words that Cleopatra uses when talking about her former lovers have sexual associations – *stand, grow* and *die*. In Elizabethan English *die* referred to a sexual climax. ✪ Look at Enobarbus's speech in Act 1, scene 2 beginning *Under a compelling occasion* ... What is the effect of the frequent references to *dying*? What do they tell you about Enobarbus, and about Cleopatra?

Over to you

? Skim-read scenes 1–3. Underline all the references to Caesar. What impression of Caesar do you receive before he appears in person?

? Find examples in which Cleopatra is shown to be:

clever   playful   loving   sexual   emotional
cruel   insecure   puzzling

? Make a rough design of a set showing how you would present Rome and Egypt on the stage.

? Look at this way of remembering some of the key aspects of Rome and Egypt. You could copy and illustrate this mnemonic, or make up one of your own.

R – rigour	**E** – excess
O – order	**G** – glamour
M – moderation	**Y** – youthfulness
E – efficiency	**P** – pleasure
	T – transcendental love

? Who:
ate strange flesh?
is *the triple pillar of the world*?
gets money where/ He loses hearts?
will outlive the lady she serves?

How will the first meeting of Caesar and Antony go? Have a break before finding out.

Act 2 scene 1

Confrontation ahead

◆ Pompey assesses the power of the triumvirate.
◆ He hopes that Antony will remain in Egypt.
◆ He is dismayed to hear that Antony is on his way to Rome.

Pompey is confident of his power at sea, and of his popular support. He accurately assesses the weakness of the triumvirate: Antony is distracted in Egypt; Caesar does not have the people's affection; Lepidus is of little real importance.
○ Which of the three men does Pompey see as the greatest threat?

Pompey dismisses the messenger's news that Caesar and Lepidus are ready for battle, but further news that Antony will soon be in Rome forces him to consider the strength of a newly reconciled triumvirate. Pompey thinks that the threat of his growing power may cause Antony and Caesar to *cement their divisions and bind up/ The petty difference*. Pompey's pride is bolstered by the thought that he is dangerous enough to cause the great soldier Mark Antony to return to Rome.
○ What impression do you receive of Pompey? What are Antony's reasons for returning to Rome?

Pompey admires Antony's military prowess – *His soldiership is twice the other twain* – and he knows that Antony's active presence in Rome threatens his own success. Like other Romans, he speaks mockingly of Antony the *libertine*, hoping that his love of pleasure will keep him in Egypt and that his sense of honour will be more and more dulled by feasting and drinking. Cleopatra is beautiful, lustful and associated with witchcraft. She has the power to trap and enchant Antony.

Menas and Menacretes are Pompey's officers, *famous pirates* who on his behalf fight for control of the sea, capturing ship after ship. ❂ Look at the map on p. 7. Why is command of the sea important?

Act 2 scene 2

Reconciliation

◆ Antony, Caesar and Lepidus meet in Rome.
◆ They agree to unite to fight Pompey.
◆ Antony agrees to marry Caesar's sister, Octavia.
◆ The triumvirate decide to move against Pompey after the marriage.
◆ Enobarbus tells the Roman soldiers about Cleopatra.

Face to face

 Lepidus acts as peacemaker, asking Enobarbus to persuade Antony to be conciliatory, not angry. Enobarbus's refusal to intervene in this way and his staunch support of Antony's position emphasize the tense atmosphere and how difficult it will be to achieve and maintain friendship and unity.

Tension is maintained as Caesar and Antony enter from different sides of the stage, each ostentatiously deep in discussion with his officer, not wishing to make the first approach. Lepidus is the mediator, and his diplomatic plea that they should not let trivial matters force them apart enables Caesar and Antony, with stiff formality, to exchange greetings and to take their seats.

Antony takes the initiative, confronting Caesar with his misinterpretation of his (Antony's) behaviour. Caesar moves into a series of accusations: Antony plotted with Fulvia and her brother Lucius in their war against Caesar; he ignored Caesar's messages and treated his messenger contemptuously; he broke his oath by refusing to supply Caesar with troops and arms when he required them. ❂ Which of these accusations is most important to Antony?

45

Antony denies any responsibility for Fulvia's machinations, saying that she was uncontrollable, and that in any case a war against Caesar was a war against Antony as well, as *partner in the cause.* He acknowledges that when he was in Egypt *poisoned hours* caused him to neglect his duty, and apologizes for his failings in this respect. ✪ How convincing do you find Antony's responses? To what extent does he blame himself? Does either man come off better in this exchange? How far does each engage the audience's sympathy here?

Enobarbus's cynical aside about Fulvia, and the anxious, placatory interjections of Lepidus and Maecenas emphasize the underlying tension. Enobarbus's tart suggestion that Caesar and Antony can have a temporary truce in order to deal with Pompey makes Antony angry, but Caesar acknowledges that essential differences between Antony and himself will make lasting friendship difficult. ✪ What is the effect of Enobarbus's comments? Why does Antony tell him to keep quiet?

An arranged marriage

Agrippa suggests that a marriage between Antony and Caesar's sister Octavia will make their friendship secure. ✪ Has Caesar arranged for Agrippa to make this suggestion? What is Antony's immediate response? Why does he agree to the proposal? Elizabethan and Jacobean audiences would have been very familiar with the idea of marriages in important families being arranged for political or dynastic reasons. The use of Octavia as a political pawn illustrates the difference between Roman values of heartless expediency and Egyptian associations of love and emotion. ✪ What do you think of Antony's behaviour here? Is he right to deny that Cleopatra has a claim on him, and to use his overwhelming passion for her as an excuse for his behaviour? However you judge Antony at this point, it does seem that he has been out-manoeuvred by Caesar. ✪ What would have happened if he had refused the marriage? What is likely to happen if Antony does not treat Octavia well?

You should have been there!

In contrast to the cold world of Roman politics, the thrilling exoticism and magnificence of Egypt are evoked through Enobarbus's description of the first meeting of Antony and Cleopatra. This is preceded by a change of subject and tone as the leaders of the world depart and leave their officers to gossip about Egypt. ✪ What change in style do you notice? Enobarbus enjoys impressing his colleagues with his first-hand experience of the way of life which is the object of rumour and fascination. He boasts of and exaggerates the extent of their drinking and feasting in Egypt, then, prompted by the speculative comments about Cleopatra from Maecenas and Agrippa, presents a lyrical, poetic account of the lovers' meeting on the River Cydnus. Enobarbus describes the spectacle of Cleopatra sailing down the river in her royal barge, magnificently set off by the golden barge, the silver oars and the purple sails. She is attended by young boys who fan her and her women attendants who appear to be mermaids or sea nymphs, and whose graceful movements as they tend the perfumed sails and the ropes provide a beautiful frame for the wonderful centrepiece. The whole city is enthralled by this sight, and Antony is unable to resist the lure of the bewitching queen. ✪ What is the effect of the cynical, plain-spoken Enobarbus giving such an intensely poetical description?

In this description Cleopatra presents herself almost like a painting. Her appearance is staged, with every detail calculated for its effect. A more robust, dynamic picture emerges as the soldiers continue to dwell on Cleopatra's magnetic charm, with Agrippa recalling her sexual exploits with Julius Caesar and Enobarbus describing how she hopped forty paces through the public street and made even her breathlessness seem to be part of her perfection. Just the spellbinding sight on the Cydnus is a combination of art and nature, so Cleopatra combines royalty and earthiness, nature and artifice; she is both *royal* and a *wench.* Enobarbus admires her *infinite variety.* ✪ What variety do you find in Cleopatra? The scene finishes with Maecenas presenting the Roman party line, praising Octavia's *beauty, wisdom* and *modesty.* ✪ What is the effect, at this point, of such a description of Octavia?

STYLE AND LANGUAGE

The speech beginning *The barge she sat in* is a striking contrast to the prose which precedes it. Its pulsing iambic rhythm has an almost hypnotic effect, similar to the effect Cleopatra has on those watching. The **simile** in which the boat, glowing in the sun's fiery rays, is compared to a throne is enhanced by the **alliteration** in *barge, burnished, burned.* An impression of seductive softness is created by the alliteration in *poop, purple, perfumed*, and the eroticism is developed in the **metaphors** of the winds being *lovesick* with the sails, and the love affair between the oars and the water. We are prepared for the appearance of Cleopatra, a magnificent piece of stage-management, as she displays herself in a manner reminiscent of an elaborate painting of the goddess Venus – but even more stunning. Cleopatra's beauty surpasses even the best that can be created by art improving on nature. Her beauty is enhanced by the *glow* on her *delicate cheeks*, which is created by the fans intended to cool her, another example of **paradox**. The alliteration in *seeming, silken, swell* adds to the sensuous effect, which is intensified by further reference to the *strange invisible perfume.*

✪ Where does this passage appeal to the senses of smell, touch, sight, sound, and hearing? Why is Cleopatra frequently described in paradoxical terms? Note that images which appeal to the senses are easier to remember than abstract ideas: incorporate images in your revision techniques.

Act 2 scene 3

A promise and a prophecy

◆ Antony promises Octavia that he will behave better in future.
◆ A soothsayer predicts that Caesar will be more successful than Antony.
◆ Antony decides to go back to Egypt.

Antony prepares Octavia for his frequent absences, and asks her not to believe the bad rumours about him. He admits in the past he has not been guided by the *square*, but promises that in the future he will follow the *rule*. ✪ What impression is created by the imagery of carpenters' tools? Is this imagery 'Roman' or 'Egyptian'? What impression is created by the entrance of Octavia between Caesar and Antony?

The soothsayer says that Caesar has *natural luck*, and that he will always overshadow Antony. Antony's brilliance and his noble spirit are diminished when he is with Caesar. ✪ How true is this claim? In Act 2, scene 2, how far were Antony's good qualities eclipsed by Caesar? In his soliloquy, Antony agrees with the soothsayer's assessment. He remarks on Caesar's lucky touch – *The very dice obey him* – and muses that Antony's *better cunning* cannot bring him success. The soothsayer has suggested that Antony should return to Egypt. ✪ What personal reasons might the soothsayer have for suggesting this? (Look at his first words: *Would I had never come from thence* [Egypt].)

Antony seizes on the comments about Caesar, using them as a justification for leaving Rome and returning to Egypt, where, out of Caesar's way, his *lustre* will shine. ✪ Is Antony looking for an excuse? In the space of forty lines, he has gone from promising to be a good husband to Octavia, to deciding: *I will to Egypt; And though I make this marriage for my peace,/ I'th'East my pleasure lies.* ✪ Is Antony's decision based on his fear of being overshadowed by his younger rival, or on his passion for Cleopatra? What will he be sacrificing if he leaves Rome? What will he be sacrificing if he stays in Rome? The use of the soothsayer suggests that events are inevitable and beyond the control of individuals. ✪ How true is this?

Act 2 scene 4

Preparations for war

◆ Lepidus, Agrippa and Maecenas prepare to travel to Misenum.
◆ They will meet Caesar and Antony there.

This short scene reminds the audience of the political conflict, and creates a sense of urgency and purposeful movement. Positioned between depictions of Antony's decision to go back to Egypt, and Cleopatra's listlessness in his absence, the scene helps to keep us aware of what is at stake.

Exercise your brain muscles

? Which of the following words describe Antony, and which describe Caesar? Some words may apply to both. Start a Mind Map of the similarities and differences between Caesar and Antony.

emotional   rational   self-doubting   certain
confused   defensive   dignified   self-controlled
ambitious   self-righteous

? Think of a piece of music to accompany Enobarbus's description of Cleopatra in the barge.

? Which of these characters do you admire most at this point in the play, and which least? Put them in order, and explain your reasons. You could exchange ideas with a friend.

Caesar   Antony   Pompey   Lepidus

? How strongly do you agree with the following statements? Mark each on a five-point scale.

The Romans are fascinated by Cleopatra.
The Romans despise Cleopatra.
The Romans fear Cleopatra.

How would you like to be the one to tell Cleopatra that Antony is married? Have a short break, then find out how she takes the news!

Act 2 scene 5

He's married someone else!

◆ Cleopatra hears that Antony is married.
◆ She attacks the messenger.

Cleopatra's restlessness and moodiness are evident at the beginning of the scene as she calls for music, changes her mind, thinks that billiards will distract her, then changes her mind again. The bawdy joking with Mardian, in which Cleopatra bemoans his lack of sexual ability, leads into reminiscences of her time with Antony. Cleopatra recalls the playful nature of their fishing expeditions, how she tricked Antony into thinking that he had caught a big fish, and how she teased him until he lost patience, then teased him back into a good humour. She would imagine that every fish she drew up was Antony, hooked and captured by her. ○ What range of emotions does Cleopatra display here? How sympathetic do you find her?

The description of Cleopatra dressing Antony in her *tires* [head-dresses] *and mantles* while she wears his *sword Philippan* reminds us of Caesar's complaint that Antony has become *womanly*. ○ What is suggested by the image of Cleopatra taking away Antony's sword? What are the associations of *sword*?

The atmosphere becomes charged with tension as the messenger enters, the **dramatic irony** of the situation increasing the audience's expectations. The fiercely sexual image *Ram thou thy fruitful tidings in mine ears/ That long time have been barren* emphasizes Cleopatra's passion and desire. ○ What do you think the messenger is feeling at this point? The drama of the scene is laced with comedy and pathos as Cleopatra tries to anticipate what the messenger will say, alternately pleading with him and threatening him, and he tries to get a word in edgeways. The sweeping generosity of her offer to shower the messenger with gold and pearls if he reports that Antony is *well and free* is matched by the high melodrama of her threat to melt and pour the gold down his throat if he brings news that Antony is dead. Cleopatra reasserts her nobility with the reference to her bluest veins and the reminder that kings have trembled in her presence; later in the scene she upbraids herself for behaving without nobility by striking the messenger. When the messenger finally manages to blurt out the news that Antony is married, Cleopatra explodes into violence, physically attacking the messenger and threatening him with a knife. Her language is also violent and histrionic: *Thou shalt be whipped with wire, and stewed in brine,/ Smarting in ling'ring pickle!* ✪ What is your response to this part of the scene? How far is Cleopatra's behaviour justified by the depth of her feelings?

Cleopatra finally has to accept the fact that Antony is married, and the scene finishes on a subdued note, focusing on Cleopatra's vulnerability and her confused, ambivalent emotions as she asks for a description of Octavia, and wavers between seeing Antony as a hateful figure, the Gorgon, and as Mars, the great god of war. The Gorgon is a mythical female monster whose glance turns people to stone. ✪ Why does she compare him to a *female* monster? How does the whole scene affect your judgement of Cleopatra? What new aspects of her personality are revealed?

Act 2 scene 6

Making peace with Pompey

◆ Caesar, Antony and Lepidus negotiate with Pompey.
◆ Pompey agrees to their terms.
◆ Enobarbus predicts that Antony will go back to Cleopatra.

The confrontation with Pompey reveals the personalities of the participants and their interpersonal rivalries. Pompey appears as a lightweight figure in spite of the lofty words with which he gives his reasons for taking up arms against the triumvirate: *To scourge th'ingratitude that despiteful Rome/ Cast on my noble father.* He has opposed them because of their support of Julius Caesar, who clashed with Pompey's father (Pompey the Great) in the civil war. However, Pompey's personal motivation seems to count for at least as much as his political position. He accuses Antony of having cheated in a transaction to buy Pompey the Great's house, and of having shown insufficient gratitude for favours done for him by Pompey's mother. Having accepted Antony's belated thanks he then agrees to the terms of the treaty, accepting Sicily and Sardinia in return for ridding the sea of pirates and sending wheat to Rome. ❂ Why does Pompey accept the treaty? Once peace has been agreed, Pompey calls for a feast to celebrate, referring to the *fine Egyptian cookery* that Antony has enjoyed, then tactlessly refers to Cleopatra's former affair with Julius Caesar. ❂ Can you think of any reasons for Pompey's behaviour? What makes him appear out of his depth when dealing with the triumvirate?

Caesar says little, but his words are to the point and aimed at getting results. He allows Pompey to put his case – *Take your time* – but maintains focus on the business in hand: *There's the point* and *That's the next to do.* His advice to Pompey should he wish *To try a larger fortune* could be a warning to Pompey not to take further action against them, or it could be a promise of greater gains if he joins them. ❂ How is this ambiguity typical of Caesar?

Antony's previous actions nearly prevent the signing of the treaty, or so Pompey claims. He offers Pompey *liberal thanks*, and his openness and generosity are seen in his frank acknowledgement that Pompey's actions have caused him to leave the soft beds in the East. However, Antony's personal warmth is overshadowed by Caesar's skilful politicking. ❂ How prominent is Lepidus in this scene? How successful would the triumvirate be if they faced a more formidable opponent than Pompey?

Soldiers' talk

The blunt prose of Menas and Enobarbus, former enemies drawn on to the same side by the new treaty, provides a cynical, realistic comment on the behaviour of the world leaders, and reveals the uncertainties and weaknesses behind the alliance. Menas's observation that Pompey *doth this day laugh away his fortune* highlights Pompey's poor judgement. ❂ What different emotions might Menas feel at this point? The soldiers' recognition of the political nature of the marriage between Antony and Octavia heightens our awareness of the fragility of the peace it has bought. Enobarbus's prediction that Antony *will to his Egyptian dish again* increases the tension; it will not be long before Octavia, *the band that seems to tie their friendship together*, becomes the *strangler of their amity*. ✪ With whom do you sympathize more, Antony or Octavia? What is the tone of Enobarbus's reference to the *Egyptian dish*? Look at the description of Octavia: *holy, cold and still*. How does this description affect your view of Octavia and of Cleopatra?

Act 2 scene 7

A feast on the galley

◆ Pompey hosts a feast on his ship.
◆ Menas suggests that Pompey should kill the triumvirs and become leader.
◆ Menas decides to leave Pompey.
◆ Caesar leaves early.

A light-hearted atmosphere is created as the servants mock Lepidus, out of his depth, drunk, and trying to keep the peace between the others. The comic effect is increased by Antony's humouring his drunken partner's incoherent comments about Egypt. The frivolity is undercut when Menas whispers to Pompey that he has an ideal opportunity to kill Caesar, Antony and Lepidus and become *lord of the whole world*. Pompey says that if Menas had done the deed without telling him, it would have been *good service*, but he cannot sanction the action without violating his *honour*. ✪ What do you think of Pompey's idea of honour? How is it different from Antony's? What different kinds of honour exist in Rome?

Pompey's refusal to take advantage of the opportunity causes Menas to desert him. ✪ What do you think of this decision? How different and how similar are the relationships between Pompey and Menas, and Antony and Enobarbus? What examples of loyalty are there in Rome? What examples are there in Egypt?

Nearly as good as Egypt!

The drunken revelry increases as the banquet *ripens towards* an Alexandrian feast. ❍ What aspects of this scene remind you of Egypt? The feast is intended to celebrate the new alliance, but it reveals the underlying cracks and fundamental differences between the partners. Caesar's dislike of excess and loss of control cause him to reject Antony's injunction to *Be a child o'th'time*. Caesar hates the fact that the wine makes him slur his words and has made them all behave foolishly. He is mindful of the *graver business* that they have in hand. Antony, on the other hand, wants to immerse himself in pleasure until the *conquering wine* makes him forget everything. ❍ How do you respond to this contrast between the two men? Is either presented entirely sympathetically, or entirely unsympathetically?

When Lepidus finally collapses, Enobarbus's caustic humour points out the irony of the *third part of the world* being carried out drunk, and draws our attention to the undisciplined, dishonourable behaviour of the great leaders. The world of politics is marked by deceit and treachery. ❍ How does this affect your view of Antony and Cleopatra's world of love?

Pull it all together

❓ Think up one sentence that might be spoken about Cleopatra by (a) the messenger, (b) Octavia, (c) Pompey.

❓ Write notes for the actors playing Charmian, Iras and Alexas about how they should react in Act 2, scene 5, when Cleopatra receives the news of Antony's marriage.

❓ Design a flag for Rome, and a flag for Egypt.

❓ Fill in the thought bubbles overleaf for Antony, Caesar, Lepidus and Pompey as they negotiate the treaty.

❓ Who is said to be:
   a *cuckoo*?
   a *great thief by sea*?
   a *Gorgon*?
   a *strong fellow*?
   the *third part of the world*?

Act 3 scene 1

Keep the boss happy

◆ Ventidius, Antony's lieutenant, has defeated the Parthians.
◆ He decides not to press for further victory.
◆ He will give Antony the credit for this victory.

The picture of the leaders of the world stumbling off
Pompey's galley is immediately followed by the
triumphant entry of Ventidius bearing the dead body of
Pacorus, killed in revenge for the defeat of a Roman consul.
The courage and discretion of Ventidius, an ordinary soldier, is
an ironic contrast to the shabby dealings of his superiors.
Ventidius rejects Silius's suggestion to press his victory home.
He realizes that it would not be a good move to be seen to
achieve too much and outshine his master; this is what
happened to another lieutenant, who fell out of favour with
Antony for being too successful. Both Caesar and Antony have
ever won more in their officer than person. They are envious

of others' success, and protective of their own reputations.
○ How does this scene affect your view of Antony and of
Caesar? What would you say to a director of the play who
wanted to leave out this scene on the grounds that it does not
add to the main action?

Act 3 scene 2

Big men don't cry

◆ Antony and Octavia prepare to go to Athens.
◆ They bid farewell to Caesar.
◆ Enobarbus and Agrippa mock their leaders' behaviour.

Enobarbus and Agrippa deride the way Lepidus flatters
Antony and Caesar. They compare him to a lovesick girl,
echoing his fulsome praise in a mocking chorus. The
extravagant language of flattery contrasts with Enobarbus's terse
summary: *They have dispatched with Pompey; he is gone.*

Caesar's parting words to Antony convey a warning to treat
Octavia well. She should be the cement that binds the
relationship between Antony and Caesar, and should not become
the *ram to batter the fortress of it.* The forcefulness of this image
highlights the fragility of the bond between the two men.

Enobarbus remarks that it would be unmanly for Caesar
to weep on parting from Octavia; he is cynical about the
tears that Antony shed at the deaths of his opponents, Julius
Caesar and Brutus. **○** What do you think about Enobarbus's
attitude to these shows of emotion? Is it demeaning or
unmanly for a great leader to cry? Enobarbus says that
Antony's tears made him weep as well. In what tone of voice
would he say this? What does his reaction suggest about the
world of reason and the world of emotion?

STYLE AND LANGUAGE

Octavia's unenviable position, poised between loyalty to her
brother and her husband, is captured in the image:

– *the swansdown feather,*
That stands upon the swell at the full of tide,
And neither way inclines.

Her helplessness is conveyed by the picture of the delicate feather maintaining a precarious balance on the crest of a wave, soon to be pulled in one direction when the tide turns. Octavia's tears are like April showers. ❂ In Act 1, scene 2 Enobarbus likened Cleopatra's *sighs and tears* to *winds and waters*. What is the effect of the contrast between Octavia and Cleopatra?

Act 3 scene 3

What's she like?

◆ Cleopatra asks the messenger to describe Octavia.
◆ She is pleased with the messenger's report.

The scene is a mixture of comedy and pathos as the messenger, anxious to escape another attack, describes Octavia in unflattering terms, and Cleopatra twists his words to create an even more unflattering picture of her rival. The beginning of the scene, when Alexas reports that the messenger is scared to approach, reminds us of Cleopatra's tempestuous anger and of her power. However, her political dependence on Antony is revealed as she realizes that without him she could not exercise the power to have Herod's head. Cleopatra leads the messenger into giving the correct answer when she enquires if Octavia has majesty in her gait, reminding him that he is in the presence of real majesty. Cleopatra is satisfied that Octavia is *dull of tongue and dwarfish*, that she moves in a self-effacing way, and that she has a round face and a low forehead (characteristics denoting ugliness and stupidity). ❂ Look at the previous scene. How true of Octavia is the messenger's report? How does the dialogue between Cleopatra and the messenger affect your view of her?

Close companions

Cleopatra's relationship with her servants reveals aspects of her character. Charmian's interjections throughout this scene show her support of and sympathy for her mistress, culminating in her final assertion of Cleopatra's majesty and her reassuring agreement that everything will be all right. ✪ What do you learn about Cleopatra from her relationships with Charmian, Iras and Alexas?

Review and rest

? Make a chart of the pros and cons of being one of Antony's lieutenants.

? What qualities does a personal attendant of Cleopatra need to display? Make up a profile to include in an advertisement for the position.

? How should Octavia move and speak in Act 3, scene 2? Write short notes for the actor.

What are the odds that Antony and Caesar will remain in harmony? Take a short break before finding out if you were right!

Act 3 scene 4

That didn't last long!

◆ In Athens, Antony complains to Octavia about Caesar's behaviour.

◆ Octavia asks Antony not to be angry.

◆ She offers to be a mediator between Antony and Caesar.

Antony is angry and bitter that Caesar has broken the treaty with Pompey, that he has publicly disparaged Antony and only reluctantly given him the credit he feels was due, and that he has curried favour with the people by leaving them money in his will. ✪ How likely is it that Caesar is pursuing his own ambitions? Octavia's loyalties are divided between her husband and her brother. If she prays for victory for one of them, she is praying for defeat for the other.

Octavia's role as peacemaker is seen in her plea to Antony not to believe everything he hears and not to take it to heart, and in her offer to go to Rome to try to bring about a reconciliation between Antony and Caesar. ❸ How do you interpret Antony's advice to Octavia to support the one who will protect her, and his comment that she should not support whoever started the rift? Antony says that his honour is at stake. ❸ In which earlier scene did Antony defend his honour? How 'honourable' is Antony's behaviour? Might there be another reason for his allowing Octavia to leave Athens?

We are reminded that much more than a personal quarrel is at stake. Octavia's observation that a war between Antony and Caesar would cause the world to split, with the bodies of dead men filling in the crack, helps to keep in the foreground the universal scope of the action.

Act 3 scene 5

'A pair of chaps'

◆ Eros tells Enobarbus that Caesar has imprisoned Lepidus.
◆ One of Antony's officers has murdered Pompey.
◆ Antony's navy is ready to attack Caesar.

The stage is set for a confrontation between Caesar and Antony. Caesar has ruthlessly removed the obstacles to his single command of the Roman Empire. He has fought Pompey, breaking the terms of the treaty. He has made use of Lepidus in the war against Pompey, then trumped up accusations against him and had him thrown in prison. Enobarbus's description of the inevitable struggle between Caesar and Antony as a pair of jaws that will grind against each other until the world is devoured presents the two leaders as dogs fighting over food. ❸ What does this image suggest about the pursuit of power?

This scene presents Caesar's treachery and ambition, and maintains the balance of sympathy towards Antony. Although Antony has said that he will return to Cleopatra, he has not yet deserted Octavia. ❸ How may Caesar exploit the situation if Antony does leave Octavia? Can Antony be true to himself without playing into Caesar's hands? Think about the aspects of Antony's character that make him vulnerable. Is Caesar a greater or lesser person than Antony? Is Caesar a greater or lesser politician than Antony?

Act 3 scene 6

He's gone back to Cleopatra

◆ In Rome, Caesar tells his followers about Antony's behaviour in Alexandria.

◆ Octavia arrives on her peacemaking mission.

 Antony has returned to Cleopatra and made a public display of his personal and political commitment to her. Caesar's anger and outrage are evident in his first words: *Contemning Rome.* In an elaborate ceremony smacking of Egyptian extravagance and excess, Antony enthroned himself and Cleopatra on a *tribunal silvered* in *chairs of gold,* with Cleopatra dressed as the goddess Isis. They were surrounded by Cleopatra's son by Julius Caesar and their children, described with tight-lipped disapproval by Caesar as the *unlawful issue of their lust.* ✪ What aspects of this display would anger the Roman people? Making good his earlier promise to extend Cleopatra's throne with kingdoms, Antony bestows on her and her children vast areas of the Roman Empire. As Caesar lists the names of countries and provinces, the outrage at Antony's presumption and at his betrayal of Rome increases. ✪ How justified is Caesar's self-righteousness? How has he himself shown contempt for Rome?

Caesar reports Antony's accusations against him, and his replies. Antony alleges that Caesar owes him ships, that Caesar has not given him his share of Pompey's territories, and that it was wrong of Caesar to depose Lepidus and confiscate his belongings. ✪ What do you think of Caesar's answer that Lepidus had grown too cruel and abused his authority? How has Lepidus been depicted? Caesar offers Antony conditions of peace that he knows Antony will not accept. ✪ Does Caesar really want peace with Antony?

'Like a market maid'

Caesar seems angry that Octavia arrives without pomp and ceremony. He exaggerates the types of display that should have accompanied her visit: as Caesar's sister, she should have an army for an usher, whose dust should have *ascended to the roof of heaven.* ✪ How typical of Caesar is this use of hyperbole? What reaction does he want to arouse? Why would Caesar have liked the opportunity of giving Octavia an ostentatious welcome? The description of Octavia's unobtrusive arrival contrasts sharply with the picture of Cleopatra at the beginning of the scene. ✪ How is it in Caesar's interests to present Octavia as the innocent, abused wife?

Caesar wastes no time in informing Octavia of Antony's behaviour. He milks the situation to his advantage, using the seemingly innocent question *Where is he now?* as a springboard for a damning account of Antony's actions, in which Caesar shows little consideration for his sister's feelings, but bluntly states that Antony hath *given his empire/ Up to a whore.* The extent of Antony's power is displayed in the roll call of the *kings o'th'earth* whose support Antony has enlisted. As each name is heard we receive the impression of a mighty force drawn from a huge range of territories. ✪ How will the Roman people respond to this list? How will they respond to the reinforcement of Cleopatra as a whore and Antony as a whore's fool?

In Act 2, scene 3, the soothsayer speaks of Caesar's *natural luck*; here Caesar speaks of letting *determined things* take their destined course. ✪ How far does Caesar make his own luck? Look at the way he is always ahead of the game. In response to Agrippa's advice to answer Antony's accusations he says *'Tis done already*, and he tells Octavia that he knows everything Antony is up to: *I have eyes upon him/ And his affairs come to me on the wind.* Caesar can behave ruthlessly in pursuit of his aims. ✪ Think of two examples where Caesar makes use of people for political and military purposes before turning against them.

Your turn

❓ Put these events in the order in which they occur:

(a) Octavia visits Caesar in Rome (b) Caesar gets rid of Lepidus (c) Antony returns to Egypt (d) Caesar breaks the treaty with Pompey.

? Put the above events in a different order. How does the new sequence affect your view of the conflict between Antony and Caesar?

? Find on the map on p. 7 the kingdoms that Antony gives to Cleopatra.

? Who is:

> *Dull of tongue and dwarfish?*
>
> *troubled with the green-sickness?*
>
> *troubled with a rheum?*
>
> *Half afear'd to come?*
>
> *a piece of virtue?*

? Find places where Cleopatra is:

> impatient   triumphant   reassured   proud
> uncertain   jealous

? Write short notes for the actors playing Charmian and Iras in the scene where Cleopatra hears that Antony is married.

Nothing can stop the confrontation between Antony and Caesar. Have a break before entering battle.

Act 3 scene 7

A disastrous decision

◆ Enobarbus objects to Cleopatra's presence in the battle.
◆ Caesar's forces are moving quickly.
◆ Antony decides to fight Caesar by sea.

Enobarbus is strongly opposed to Cleopatra's personally taking part in the battle. He fears that she will distract Antony, and his professional pride is wounded by the mocking comments being made in Rome that Cleopatra's eunuchs and maidservants are running the war. Enobarbus comments bluntly that having stallions and mares fighting together is asking for trouble. ✪ What is the effect of this image? Cleopatra insists that she has a personal stake in the battle, and has a right to be there as *president of my kingdom*. She asserts her position as head of state, in contrast to Enobarbus's focus on her gender and sexual identity.

The debate about whether to fight by sea or land is punctuated by news of Caesar's speedy and successful manoeuvres, in the face of which Antony's military strategies appear clumsy and ill considered. His declaration that he will fight by sea has the ring of bluster and bravado, and is an emotional response to Caesar's challenge. ✪ What feelings influence Antony to make this response? Can you understand his feelings?

The foolhardiness of the decision is highlighted by the stunned response of his soldiers. Canidius, Enobarbus and an ordinary soldier present a succession of pleas to Antony to reconsider. Their reasons are compelling. Antony's strength is in his land army, and he has *renowned knowledge* of fighting on land. His navy, on the other hand, consists of inexperienced sailors and clumsy ships. The desperate plea of the soldier: *O noble emperor, do not fight by sea,/ Trust not to rotten planks* illustrates how the highest to the lowest ranks are alarmed at Antony's decision. Yet Antony stubbornly refuses to change his mind. ✪ Caesar has ignored challenges that Antony has given him, but Antony responds to Caesar's challenge here. What differences between Caesar and Antony does this reveal? Why does Cleopatra support Antony's decision?

The discussion at the end of the scene shows the soldiers' dismay. They are staggered at how quickly Caesar's fleet has crossed the sea and established itself at Toryne, and at how Caesar has managed to fool Antony's spies. ✪ What is their attitude to Caesar? Antony has turned them into *women's men*. ✪ Is it true that Antony is being led by Cleopatra?

Act 3 scenes 8 and 9

Ready for battle

◆ Caesar tells his lieutenant not to strike by land until the sea battle is over.
◆ Antony tells Enobarbus to put his squadrons on a hillside to observe Caesar's fleet.

These two short scenes plunge us into the battle, and illustrate the differences between the two commanders. Caesar gives crisp instructions to Taurus not to fight by land until the sea battle is over. He orders his lieutenant to follow precisely the written instructions he has prepared. Antony's preparations are far less advanced. He wants to assess the strength of Caesar's fleet before making a move. ✪ What outcome does each expect here? What qualities does each display?

Act 3 scene 10

Running away

◆ Cleopatra flees from the battle.
◆ Antony follows her.
◆ Canidius moves over to Caesar's side.
◆ Enobarbus wavers but decides to stay with Antony.

The sight of Cleopatra's flagship sailing away from the battle, with sixty ships following, distresses Enobarbus so much that he cannot bear to watch. His anger is echoed by Scarus, who bitterly denounces Cleopatra: *Yon ribraudred nag of Egypt/ Whom leprosy o'ertake.* He describes how, the battle being even with Antony having the slight advantage, Cleopatra flees the battle *like a cow in June.* Antony follows *like a doting mallard.* ✪ What is the effect of the animal and disease imagery?

Scarus is beside himself with rage and disappointment. Antony's shameful act has violated *Experience, manhood, honour.* The great captain has let himself and his army down; he has become *the noble ruin of her magic.* Scarus blames Antony's defeat on Cleopatra. ✪ Is he right to do so? Is Antony's nobility in ruins? What different ways are there of interpreting *nobility*?

65

Should I stay or should I go?

The effects of Antony's action are seen in Canidius's declaration that Antony's flight has encouraged his followers to do the same. He is ready to desert to Caesar, as six kings have already done. Enobarbus's reason tells him that he should leave Antony, but he decides to stay. ✪ What do you think about Enobarbus's decision?

Act 3 scene 11

Shame and disgrace

◆ Antony is ashamed of his behaviour.
◆ He tells his followers to leave him and go to Caesar.
◆ Cleopatra begs Antony's pardon.
◆ Antony forgives her.

Antony is deeply ashamed and full of self-disgust. The image of a traveller overtaken by darkness on his journey conveys his sense of failure and confusion. Antony the *noble* is devastated by his dishonourable behaviour. In military and personal terms, he has *lost command*, and he hints that he will take his own life. However, even in defeat and at his lowest ebb, Antony portrays the qualities that make him such a charismatic leader and figurehead. With a different kind of nobility, he demonstrates self-awareness and the warm magnanimity which inspires loyal devotion. He urges his friends to leave him, promising to make it easy for them to join Caesar, and urging them to take his treasure. ✪ What do Antony's followers feel at this point? How do you respond to Antony here?

Overwhelmed by a sense of his defeat, Antony addresses an imaginary listener, recalling his military success at Philippi when he defeated Cassius and Brutus, while the young, inexperienced Caesar relied on his officers to fight for him and wore his sword as an ornament, *like a dancer*.

A final choice

Eros, Iras and Charmian urge Cleopatra to approach Antony and comfort him. Antony, bitterly castigating himself for the loss of his honour and nobility, is unaware of her presence. Cleopatra is faint, according to Eros, almost to the point of death. ❂ How genuine is Cleopatra's faint? How serious is this crisis?

Antony acknowledges that he allowed Cleopatra to lead him – his heart was tied to her rudder, and her slightest gesture would cause Antony to reject even *the bidding of the gods*. Here Antony commits himself entirely to Cleopatra. He forgives her for her action, and declares that one tear is worth all that is won or lost. ❂ What do you think about Antony's definition of himself as primarily Cleopatra's lover? Will it satisfy him? Is the conflict between love and duty totally resolved? Antony achieves a different kind of nobility in defeat, but at the same time he feels that he has *offended reputation/ A most unnoble swerving*.

Antony is stung by having to demean himself before Caesar. He remembers his former greatness when he influenced *half the bulk o' the world*. ❂ How far does he blame Cleopatra for this change in his fortunes?

At the end of the scene Antony forces himself into a more buoyant mood. Sustained by Cleopatra's kiss, he calls for wine and food and defies Fortune's blows. ❂ How convincing is Antony's stand against fortune?

A workout for your mind muscles

? How might (a) a reader interested in gender issues and (b) one interested in political issues respond to Cleopatra's insistence on commanding her fleet? Write a sentence from each point of view.

? List or underline all the derogatory phrases spoken about Cleopatra in these scenes. Highlight the phrases that reflect judgement of her sexual behaviour. What do you notice?

? Cleopatra is not always certain of Antony's feelings towards her. Draw a graph to chart her fluctuating feelings.

? Write a sentence about Antony at the end of Act 3, scene 10, that might be spoken by (a) Caesar, (b) Eros, (c) the soldier.

Have a short break before seeing how Caesar treats the defeated Antony.

Act 3 scene 12

Driving a wedge between them

◆ Antony sends his schoolteacher as ambassador to Caesar.
◆ Caesar refuses Antony's requests.
◆ Caesar sends Thidias to try to win Cleopatra over from Antony.

Dolabella scornfully points out that Antony has only his low-status schoolteacher to negotiate on his behalf, a mark of how low he has fallen. Caesar brusquely dismisses Antony's request to be allowed to live in Egypt, or as a private citizen in Athens. Cleopatra puts herself in Caesar's hands and asks that her heirs should inherit the crown of Egypt. ✪ What do these requests suggest about Antony and about Cleopatra at this stage? Caesar sends a message that he will negotiate with Cleopatra on condition that she drives Antony out of Egypt, or kills him. ✪ What do you think of the way that Caesar behaves in victory? Is he acting honourably? Why does he want to get rid of Antony?

Caesar orders Thidias to promise anything to Cleopatra to separate her from Antony. He is convinced that he will succeed since all women at the best of times are weak and malleable, but in times of need they are more easily corrupted. ✪ What do you think of Caesar's attitude to women? Caesar's final command to Thidias is to report how the defeated Antony is behaving. He wants to know Antony's state of mind. ✪ What might be his reasons for wanting this information? What does this request add to your impression of Caesar?

Act 3 scene 13

A challenge to Caesar

◆ Antony receives Caesar's reply.
◆ Antony challenges Caesar to a one-to-one fight.
◆ Cleopatra negotiates with Caesar's messenger.
◆ Antony has the messenger whipped.

Cleopatra's mood is less confident at the beginning of this scene, and she questions whether she or Antony is to blame for their situation. Enobarbus is blunt and forthright. Antony made his *will/ Lord of his reason* and should not have allowed his passion for Cleopatra to influence his military behaviour. Enobarbus has a choric role in the play, guiding our responses and predicting events. ✪ Is his assertion that reason should prevail over emotion the overall impression created by the play? What is Enobarbus's own situation with regard to reason and emotion?

Antony's scornful response to Caesar's message focuses on Caesar's youth. Caesar wants Antony's *grizzled head*, and he wears the *rose of youth*. Antony's challenge of a hand-to-hand sword fight with Caesar is delivered with bluster and bravado. Enobarbus's aside offers a trenchant comment on Antony's behaviour, pointing out how unlikely it is that Caesar, the commander of great armies, will make a public exhibition of himself by fighting Antony. Enobarbus draws attention to Antony's faulty judgement, and questions his own wisdom in remaining loyal to someone acting so foolishly. ✪ What reason does he give for remaining with Antony?

Mind games

Thidias's approach to the queen lacks the respect that she has been used to. Cleopatra is put on her mettle, knowing that she will have to tread carefully in her dealings with Caesar. She says that she agrees with Caesar's assessment that she is with Antony out of fear, not love, and that her honour was *conquered merely*. ✪ Is Cleopatra being truthful? Is she playing for time? Can you tell what her real intentions are?

Enobarbus assumes that Cleopatra is betraying Antony, and leaves to inform his master of what is happening. His resolve to leave Antony is increased by this further display of Antony's waning power: *Sir, sir, thou art so leaky/ That we must leave thee to thy sinking.* Cleopatra continues to play along with Caesar's attempts to win her over, and convinces Thidias that she is genuine. ❂ What is the nature of the kiss that Thidias bestows on Cleopatra's hand? Why does she, at this point, reminisce about Julius Caesar? How far do you blame Antony for misinterpreting what he sees?

A whipping

Antony explodes with rage when he sees Thidias kissing Cleopatra's hand. His rage is exacerbated by Thidias's response that he is acting on behalf of the *fullest man.* Antony exercises his waning authority, calling for his servants to whip the messenger, overriding their reluctance to perform such an outrageous act. He is aware of his lack of power and influence, and his cry *I am Antony yet* is a pathetic assertion of his former identity. ❂ With whom is Antony most angry, Thidias, Cleopatra or his servants? With whom is he really angry?

Antony turns on Cleopatra, calling her a *kite* and cursing himself for having left Octavia for her. In a furious, emotional tirade he refers to Cleopatra's former lovers, citing them as evidence of her lustfulness and lechery. Phrases such as *morsel* and *fragment* are deliberately demeaning, and are the kind of phrase the Romans use of Cleopatra. The biblical reference to the hill of Basan suggests the intensity of Antony's anguish, as he pictures himself roaring more loudly than the *horned herd,* which refers both to the bulls on the hill and to the men whom Cleopatra has turned into cuckolds with horns.

Antony sends Thidias back to Caesar with the message that he is angry because Caesar is *proud and disdainful,* taking advantage of Antony's current situation where his *good stars* have left him. ❂ How sympathetic do you find Antony at this point? How do you react to the whipping of Thidias? What do you think of Antony's suggestion that Caesar can whip, hang or torture Antony's freed slave Hipparchus?

Making up again

Cleopatra lets Antony's rage run its course. The impetus of his outburst diminishes with the prophetic, lyrical line: *Alack, our terrine moon is now eclipsed/ And it portends alone the fall of Antony.* Cleopatra's response to his question *Cold-hearted towards me?* is moving and exalted in tone. The sweeping hyperbolic image of the destruction of herself, her children and Egypt should she prove unfaithful is powerful and forceful. Antony is convinced, and musters optimism for another fight. Reassured of Cleopatra's loyalty, he vows to be *treble-sinewed, hearted, breathed* and to *send to darkness all that stop me.* ❂ How convincing are Antony's declarations? How likely is it that he will defeat Caesar?

Antony's generosity and emotional expansiveness can be seen in his call for one more night of feasting to cheer his *sad captains.* His buoyant mood leads Cleopatra to say that she can now celebrate her birthday, *since my lord/ Is Antony again.* ❂ How does Cleopatra define Antony's identity? Antony's final words are a challenge to death and a declaration that he will make death love him.

Deserting the sinking ship

The hollowness that lies beneath Antony's words is underlined by Enobarbus's decision to leave his master. Antony's reason and judgement are diminished, and his blustering shows of courage are irrational and foolish. Enobarbus has lost faith in Antony, whose display of valour without reason will lead to destruction. ❂ How do you respond to Enobarbus's decision? How typical of him is it to follow the path of reason and good sense? Has Enobarbus shown any emotional responses in the course of the play? Is there an 'Egyptian' side to him?

✒ STYLE AND LANGUAGE

The imagery of melting and dissolution creates a sense of disintegration and uncertainty. Antony's cry *Authority melts from me* suggests that his notion of himself and his identity is slipping away. Cleopatra says that if she is cold-hearted,

71

poisoned hailstones will *dissolve* her life, and by the *discandying* of the storm of hail, all her children will die. The concept of substance shifting and changing becomes stronger as the play continues, preparing us for the deaths of Antony and Cleopatra.

More for you

? What similarities and differences are there in Antony's treatment of Thidias and Cleopatra's treatment of the messenger in Act 2, scene 5? Make a Mind Map of your ideas.

? Enobarbus compares Antony to an old dying lion. What animals would you choose to represent Antony, Cleopatra and Caesar? Explain your choice to a friend.

? Look at this way of remembering the difficult situations that Cleopatra faces in Act Three:

Many **A**ctors **C**annot **D**ance. **M** – marriage (Antony's); **A** – Actium; **C** – Caesar's messenger; **D** – despair (Antony's). Make up a mnemonic of your own to help you to remember the different locations in this act – Parthia, Rome, Athens, Egypt, Actium.

Time for a short break before more tears are shed.

Act 4 scene 1

'Poor Antony!'

◆ Caesar ridicules Antony's challenge.
◆ Caesar intends the next battle to be the decisive one.

The contrast between Caesar and Antony is marked. Caesar is cool and controlled, refusing to rise to Antony's bait. He gives instructions to *Laugh at his challenge*, and refers to Antony as the *old ruffian*. Maecenas describes Antony as a hunted animal at bay, and points out that an angry man does not defend himself well. ❂ In what ways does Antony remind you of a hunted animal?

Caesar is confident of victory – he callously notes that there are enough of Antony's deserters in his army to capture him. His arrangement for a feast to reward and motivate his army is considered and calculated, based on an assessment of expenditure and provisions, and lacks Antony's sweeping generosity. ❂ How different are the relationships that Caesar and Antony have with their followers?

Act 4 scene 2

Sad goodbyes

◆ Antony hears that Caesar has rejected his challenge.
◆ Antony addresses his servants and makes them weep.
◆ Antony assures them that he will be victorious in the next day's battle.

Antony is surprised to hear that Caesar will not fight him in single combat. ❂ Is anyone else surprised? How sound is Antony's judgement at this point? Antony is determined to regain his *dying honour* in the imminent battle. ❂ Is victory in battle the only mark of honour for Antony? In what other areas of his experience can he gain or lose honour?

Antony bids an emotional farewell to his servants, thanking them for their loyal service and asking them to wait on him this one last night. He has a powerful effect on his followers, making them feel part of his success. His easy generosity – *Be bounteous at our meal* – contrasts sharply with Caesar's cautious arrangement in the previous scene. Antony seems almost to relish the drama and melancholy of the situation as he clasps the hand of each servant and tells them that they may not see him again and may the next day serve another master. His request for them to *Tend me tonight two hours* has echoes of the New Testament account of Christ asking his apostles to keep watch one night with him (Matthew 26), and intensifies the feeling of impending doom.

Cleopatra is puzzled by Antony's behaviour, and twice asks Enobarbus what it means. Enobarbus is himself moved to tears, and remonstrates with Antony: *Transform us not to women.* ❂ What does this comment reveal about Enobarbus? Antony seems unaware of the effect of his words, and tries to joke them away. He injects a note of optimism, saying that he expects victory the next day. ❂ What is the dominant tone of this scene?

Act 4 scene 3

Hercules deserts Antony

◆ Antony's soldiers are on watch.
◆ They hear music in the air and under the earth.

The atmosphere is tense and uneasy as the soldiers keep watch. They are keyed up for the crucial battle the next day, and ask about the latest news and rumours in terse exchanges. They keep up their spirits with assurances that they have a fine army, full of resolution, which should do well if the navy holds up.

The music which fills the air is eerie and ominous. One soldier hesitantly suggests that it is a good sign, but the overwhelming impression is that the music signifies disaster. Antony's god Hercules is leaving him. His good luck is over; his fate is determined. The outcome of the battle is inevitable.

Act 4 scene 4

Buckling up

◆ Eros and Cleopatra help Antony to put on his armour.
◆ Antony sets off for battle.

The sombre mood of the previous scene gives way to an energetic atmosphere as the battle morning dawns. Cleopatra insists on helping Antony put on his armour. The gentle comedy as she makes mistakes and puts on the pieces the wrong way mingles with the more significant allusions to the couple's individual roles and identities, and Cleopatra's influence over Antony. Here, any such conflicts seem to have been resolved as Cleopatra helps Antony to assume the role of warrior in a striking visual way. With every piece of armour Antony dons, he is metamorphosed into the great captain. Cleopatra is content now not to be a participant in the battle, but to be the *armourer of my heart*. ✪ How is this scene different from the description of Antony and Cleopatra wearing each other's clothes (Act 2, scene 5)?

Antony is confident and elated. He is proud of his *royal occupation*, and communicates his enthusiasm and spirit to his men, speaking crisply and decisively. We see here the old Antony of myth and legend, ready to command his thousand men. His farewell to Cleopatra is a *soldier's kiss*, and he leaves her *like a man of steel*. However, Cleopatra's wish that Antony and Caesar had settled the war in single combat and her tentative *but now* at the end of the scene suggest that she is not hopeful about the outcome of the battle. ✪ What evidence is there to suggest that Antony is unlikely to be successful?

Act 4 scene 5

Another desertion

◆ Antony learns that Enobarbus has deserted.
◆ He sends Enobarbus's treasure after him.

Antony meets the soldier who begged him not to fight by sea, and admits to him that he was wrong and regrets his decision. Antony's humility, honesty and willingness to accept responsibility are admirable.

The news that Enobarbus has gone over to Caesar is a huge personal blow for Antony. He has lost not only a valued lieutenant but a friend, one who shared his life in Egypt and whose pithy, cynical remarks offered a pointed if not always welcome commentary on people and events. Antony's immediate response is to send Enobarbus's treasure after him, and to write him a letter of *gentle adieus and greetings*. He blames himself completely for Enobarbus's desertion, and says that his fortunes have *Corrupted honest men.* His final anguished cry of *Enobarbus!* comes from the depths of his heart, and reverberates with loss and despair.

The optimistic mood of the previous scene is shattered. Not only Enobarbus, but a number of kings as well have deserted Antony's side before the battle starts. However, at this lowest ebb in his fortunes, Antony's magnificent qualities shine through. His self-awareness, generosity and warmth, and his capacity for emotion appear at their fullest in this moment of defeat. ✪ What might this suggest about the world of the play, or Shakespeare's outlook on life?

Act 4 scene 6

'The villain of the earth'

◆ Caesar orders the deserters from Antony to be placed at the front of the lines.
◆ Enobarbus considers the fate of the other deserters.
◆ He receives his treasure from Antony.
◆ He decides to find a ditch in which to die.

Caesar's declaration that *The time of universal peace is near* looks forward to his rule as Caesar Augustus, the first Roman Emperor. The long period of peace ushered in by his reign was seen by the Elizabethans as a preparation for the coming of Christ. The references to peace and the olive intensify the allusion to the coming of Christianity. ✪ What contrasts are there between Caesar's view and a Christian view of worldly success?

Caesar's order to place Antony's deserters at the front is a shrewd military tactic. ✪ What will its effect be on Antony? How will it benefit Caesar? Do you admire Caesar for this kind of thinking?

Enobarbus has discovered that Caesar does not treat deserters well. Alexas has been hanged, Canidius and others like him are employed but not trusted. Caesar is heading for worldly success, but he appears to be cold and mean-spirited, particularly in comparison with Antony.

Even before his treasure arrives, Enobarbus regrets his decision to leave Antony. When he is faced with Antony's generosity, he is overcome with guilt and remorse. In grief and anguish, he determines to crawl into a ditch and die. Enobarbus has followed the path of reason; his decision to leave Antony was based on a sensible assessment of Antony's position and prospects.

Act 4 scene 7

Caesar retreats

◆ Antony forces Caesar's troops to retreat.
◆ Antony promises to reward Scarus for his bravery.

The mood is jubilant as Antony's military prowess is affirmed. He has confounded Caesar's (and the audience's) expectations and forced Agrippa and his army to retreat. We see why Antony commands such loyalty – his first words to Scarus show concern for his wound, and he promises to reward Scarus both for his cheerful spirit and for his courage. Scarus's address to Antony, *O my brave emperor*, shows his pleasure and pride in serving such a distinguished master. Elated with this victory, Scarus says he has room for six more gashes, and jokes about the shape of his wound. He is ready to pursue Caesar's army and attack them from behind.

Act 4 scene 8

Celebration

◆ Antony praises his troops and leads them into Alexandria.
◆ He commends Scarus's bravery to Cleopatra.
◆ Antony and Cleopatra march triumphantly through the city.

Antony's address to his men shows his characteristic warmth. He thanks them for fighting not like hired soldiers, but as if the cause were their own. Proud of their courage, he elevates his men to heroic status, saying they have all behaved like Hector, the mythical perfect warrior. His speech contains reminders of battle – *blood, wounds, honoured gashes* – and at the same time encompasses the soldiers' personal and domestic lives: *clip your wives, your friends.*

The public and the personal selves of Antony and Cleopatra coexist harmoniously in this scene. Antony is bold and confident in victory, presenting Scarus and allowing him to kiss Cleopatra's hand, and taking pleasure in her offering Scarus *An armour all of gold.* ❷ How did Antony respond previously to someone kissing Cleopatra's hand? Antony tenderly refers to Cleopatra as a *great fairy, nightingale* and *girl*, while she affirms his status with *Lord of lords.* Secure not only in victory but in Cleopatra's love, Antony can now joke about his age, and claims that he can get *goal for goal of youth.* For this moment, Antony is both the lover and the soldier, combining Egypt and Rome, achieving the unity of self which has eluded him until now, and will not be sustained.

The scene ends with a triumphant blast of trumpets and preparations for a celebration. Antony wishes that they had space to *sup together/ And drink carouses to the next day's fate.* His expansive words and gestures maintain the exuberant tone and establish Antony as the successful, charismatic leader who has beaten back his enemy. ❷ Why does Shakespeare include these scenes of victory, at this point? Is the end of the scene 'Roman' or 'Egyptian' in tone? In the meantime, what is the 'Roman' Caesar likely to be doing while Antony is feasting?

Act 4 scene 9

More die of heartbreak

◆ The sentries on watch overhear Enobarbus praying for death.
◆ Enobarbus dies.
◆ The sentries carry him away.

Enobarbus asks the moon to witness his remorse for his desertion of Antony. In a lyrical address, suffused with sadness and despair, Enobarbus asks the *sovereign mistress of true melancholy* to drench him in the poisonous night air so that he may die. He asks Antony's forgiveness, and acknowledges his former master's outstanding nobility: *Nobler than my revolt is infamous.* Enobarbus wants to be remembered by the world as *a master-leaver and a fugitive.* He dies uttering an anguished repetition of Antony's name, in an echo of Antony's earlier cry of *Enobarbus!*

The invocation of the moon brings to mind Isis, the Egyptian goddess with whom Cleopatra identifies, and also creates an awareness of the transitory nature of life. Cosmic references surround the deaths of Antony and Cleopatra, with which Enobarbus is linked through imagery and theme. In choosing to leave Antony, Enobarbus followed the dictates of a certain kind of judgement. He took a pragmatic course and ignored, or failed to recognize, deeper emotional truths. For a fatal moment, Enobarbus was blind to Antony's true magnificence and to his own feelings, and disregarded the claims of loyalty, affection and the life of the spirit. Enobarbus's death demonstrates the limitations of worldly rationalism, and the importance of spiritual and emotional values in the quest for self-fulfilment and self-realization. Enobarbus denied the emotional side of his nature, and died a lonely death in a ditch. ✪ What do you find is the major emotional impact of this scene?

Your turn

? Write a short epitaph for Enobarbus on the tombstone in the illustration.

? What qualities do you think a great military leader should have? Make a Mind Map or list. Apply each item to Caesar and to Antony, and give a star rating to show to what extent each quality is demonstrated by each of them.

? Find places in scenes 1–9 where Antony is:

generous   self-pitying   inspiring   exuberant
ashamed   sad   forgiving

Antony has won the battle but not the war. Have a short break before entering the field again.

Act 4 scene 10

I'll fight him anywhere!

◆ Antony hears that Caesar's navy is at sea.
◆ Antony decides to fight Caesar at sea.

Antony's elated mood continues. He declares that he is ready to fight Caesar *i'th'fire or i'th'air* if necessary, having already fought him by land and sea. Antony will take on Caesar in all of the elements. ✪ How do you respond to Antony's mood here? He gives order for a sea battle, and he and Scarus go to the hills near the city to watch the battle.

Act 4 scene 11

Short and to the point

◆ Caesar orders his land army not to fight unless they are attacked.
◆ Caesar knows that Antony's strongest force has been sent to fight at sea.

Caesar has led Antony into deploying his best men at sea, while he keeps his own strongest force on land, thereby regaining the advantage he had lost. **○** What differences are there between the tone of this speech and Antony's in the previous scene?

Act 4 scene 12

Betrayed	

◆ Antony goes to see whether the sea fight has begun.
◆ Scarus reveals that the omens are not favourable for Antony.
◆ Antony describes the surrender of his fleet.
◆ Antony declares revenge on Cleopatra.

Scarus's words prepare us for Antony's final defeat. A feeling of impending doom is created through the account of swallows building their nests in Cleopatra's sails, an omen which the official experts claim to be unable to interpret, but which does seem to signify disaster. Antony's mood is jumpy and changeable, very different from his previous show of confidence.

Antony's eruption of fury is sudden and dramatic. Convinced that Cleopatra has betrayed him, he calls her *foul Egyptian* and *Triple-turned whore*, his humiliation and defeat causing him to lash out at her in terms that are like those the Romans use of her. Antony believes that she has now turned from him to Caesar, and sold him to this *novice*. Cleopatra becomes the focal point of his rage and disappointment. All Antony's insecurities surface and find expression in this tirade. **○** Is there any evidence that Cleopatra has made terms with Caesar? Whose fleet does Antony see surrender?

Antony faces defeat: *Fortune and Antony part here.* Images of melting and dissolving express his loss of power, as his followers *discandy, melt their sweets/ On blossoming Caesar.* Antony sees himself as a pine tree that once towered above the others, but is now stripped of its bark, laid bare. **○** What other 'vertical' images have been associated with Antony?

When Cleopatra appears, Antony's rage has reached titanic proportions. He can only just stop himself from attacking her physically, and instead lashes out with a description of how Caesar will parade Cleopatra in front of the Romans as an object of ridicule for the commonest people and weakest fools to mock. ☉ Why does Antony include the description of Octavia? How likely is it that Octavia would behave in the way he describes?

Cleopatra flees in terror, and Antony gives himself over completely to his rage. He suffers as Hercules suffered when his wife Deianira gave him a shirt that Nessus the centaur had soaked in poisoned blood. Hercules was in such agony that he hurled Lichas, the servant who brought him the shirt, into the sea. Antony's anger is so great that it can only be expressed in these mythical terms. He wants to be taught a rage that exceeds all human rage, to experience it with the violence that would fling Lichas so high in the air that he landed on the moon. Ironically, Hercules' wife acted in innocence and had no idea that the shirt was poisoned, just as, it seems, Cleopatra is innocent of collusion with Caesar. Antony, however, is possessed by his violent emotions and is convinced that Cleopatra must die for having sold him to *the young Roman boy*.

Act 4 scene 13

A desperate ploy

◆ Cleopatra decides to lock herself in her funeral monument.
◆ She sends word to Antony that she has killed herself.

💜 Cleopatra, used to Antony's anger, recognizes that his fury now is of a different order and magnitude. As Antony has done, she uses mythological references to express the nature of his rage – he is like the huge boar foaming at the mouth that ravaged the country of Calydon, and like the Greek hero Ajax who went mad and killed himself when he failed to win the shield of Achilles.

Charmian comes up with the plan that Cleopatra should lock herself in the monument and let Antony believe that she is dead. Cleopatra seizes on the idea in a desperate attempt to get Antony back. She seems to have no idea why he is so enraged, and the extreme nature of this ruse matches the extremity of his anger. ❂ What strategies has Cleopatra used previously to keep Antony's interest? How is this occasion different?

Act 4 scene 14

A suicide attempt

◆ Antony resolves to take his own life.
◆ Mardian brings the news that Cleopatra is dead.
◆ Antony orders Eros to kill him but Eros stabs himself instead.
◆ Antony falls on his own sword, but survives.
◆ Diomedes arrives with the message that Cleopatra is alive.
◆ Antony is taken to Cleopatra.

Antony's rage has calmed, and he is in a deeply melancholy, reflective mood. Defeated by Caesar and betrayed by Cleopatra, he has lost his sense of his identity. He describes how, at sunset, the clouds in the sky seem to assume different shapes. The examples he gives reflect different aspects of his personality: a dragon, a bear, a lion, a citadel, a rock, a mountain and a horse. ❂ What does each image suggest about Antony? Even as we look, Antony says, the mass of cloud shifts and the pictures become unclear *As water is in water.* The images of dissolving and melting express Antony's inability to *hold this visible shape.* Antony's military occupation was founded on his love for Cleopatra, for whose sake he has engaged in this war, and now that the basis of his life and actions seems false, nothing holds together. His words to Mardian, *She has robbed me of my sword,* encompass his sense of military and sexual defeat. ❂ How far does Antony's definition of himself depend on how others see him, just as the shapes of the clouds are created by the perception of those who gaze at them?

Cleopatra's dead

Antony's immediate response to the news of Cleopatra's death is that his life too is over: *the long day's task is*

done/ And we must sleep. With Eros's help, he removes his armour, a mirror image of the scene where he got ready for war (Act 4, scene 4). Here, with each piece of armour and equipment that is removed, Antony becomes the private man, the individual, with his power and authority removed. The pain he is suffering is expressed in the violent language: *battery, crack.* Even a shield of seven thicknesses could not protect him. He looks forward to meeting Cleopatra in death, and asking for her forgiveness. Antony imagines himself and Cleopatra in the Underworld, *where souls do couch on flowers,* living in perpetual happiness and being the focal point of attention, outshining even the famous lovers Dido and Aeneas.

A Roman act

Antony reminds Eros that he has promised to kill his master if the moment should come. He says that since Cleopatra died he is living in dishonour, and the one way left to him to reclaim both his personal honour and his Roman virtue is to take his own life. Antony captures his past glory in the magnificent image of how he covered the sea with vast fleets of ships, like cities, and how with his sword he *Quartered the world.* The imagery expresses the graceful, godlike ease of a powerful man with the world and the elements at his command. Antony presents Eros with the contrasting picture of him being led as Caesar's captive through the streets of Rome as a way of persuading Eros to kill him. Eros's action of killing himself to escape having to kill his master is a moving testament to the devotion Antony inspires. ✪ Which characters have the most loyal followers? Is there any difference in the type and quality of loyalty shown?

Eros's suicide gives Antony an example to follow. He rushes towards death, in which he will reclaim Cleopatra, in the same way as a bridegroom rushes to embrace his bride. Antony's death combines the Roman ideals of honour and courage, and the Egyptian ideals of love and emotion.

The guards' words on beholding the wounded Antony emphasize the apocalyptic nature of the death of such a great personage. The star has fallen, and time has come to an end. The sombre, majestic ring of these words with their biblical association ('And there fell a great star from heaven': Revelation 8: 11–13) takes the focus away from the bungled nature of the suicide and keeps alive the sense of Antony's glory. Similarly, the action of Decretas in taking Antony's sword as a means of ingratiating himself with Caesar is a reminder of the meanness and brutality of the world which Antony and Cleopatra are leaving behind. ❂ What do you think of Decretas's action? What do you think of Antony's botched suicide attempt? Do you find it at all comic or ridiculous?

Cleopatra's alive

Antony shows no anger or blame when he learns of Cleopatra's deception. He just wants to be taken to her. His request to be carried to Cleopatra is simple and dignified, and he tells his guards to accept his fate and not to show sorrow.

Act 4 scene 15

The death of Antony

◆ Cleopatra says she will never leave her monument.
◆ Antony is brought to the foot of the monument and hauled up.
◆ Antony dies in Cleopatra's arms.
◆ Cleopatra says that she will kill herself.

Cleopatra refuses comforts, and wants to endure the huge sorrow caused by Antony's rejection of her and, as she now discovers, his imminent death. The sight of the dying Antony leads Cleopatra to exclaim that the sun should drop from its sphere and the earth be plunged into darkness. Antony follows his assurance that he has conquered himself and not been overcome by Caesar with a request for a last kiss, but Cleopatra will not come down from the monument and risk being captured. She asserts her determination not to be staged in Caesar's triumph and to commit suicide by *knife, drugs, serpents.* She comments that she will not put herself in the position of being looked at judgementally by Octavia. ❂ What is the effect of this speech? Does it remove the focus from Antony? Is Cleopatra hogging the limelight?

As Antony is drawn up to Cleopatra, her words *Here's sport indeed* recall earlier references to angling and similar diversions (Act 2, scene 5). ❂ What is the effect of this allusion? Antony tries to speak, but Cleopatra breaks in and wants to *rail so high* that Fortune will break her wheel and be unable to bring misery into people's lives. When Antony does manage to speak, he tells Cleopatra to look to Caesar for her honour and her safety, and to trust only Proculeius.

Antony's final speech reaffirms himself as the *greatest prince o'th'world.* He asks not to be defined by his present circumstances, but to be remembered for his *former fortunes.* He is proud to die a Roman, and finally reconciles both the Roman and Egyptian worlds as he dies in Cleopatra's arms. ❂ Could Antony have achieved such a reconciliation on earth?

Cleopatra's lament on the death of Antony is moving and eloquent. In a magnificent image of dissolution, she claims that *The crown o'th'earth doth melt.* Antony's death diminishes the universe, turning the *dull world* into a *sty.* In the lines: *O, withered is the garland of the war;/ The soldier's pole is fall'n* martial and erotic images convey the loss of worldly power and the passing of joy. Now that Antony is dead, the rest of humanity merges into one, indistinguishable. Antony set the standard for greatness, and his type will never be seen again.

Cleopatra without Antony

Cleopatra corrects her women when they address her with her royal titles. She, too, was made remarkable through Antony, and now that he is gone she is *No more but e'en a woman*, experiencing the same emotions as the lowest milkmaid. Cleopatra's humble acceptance of her common humanity shifts into an angry desire to throw her sceptre at the gods who have taken Antony away. The emotional range of her speech encompasses her as an ordinary woman and the Queen of Egypt. Cleopatra's acceptance of the finality of Antony's death is sad and muted. *Our lamp is spent*, she says, evoking again the idea of the darkening of the universe, before preparing to bury Antony. After that, she will herself behave *after the high Roman fashion* and follow Antony's example.

More for you

? Find places where Antony shows the levels of anger described by the following words, and write the word and the reference on the temperature gauge.

annoyed
irritated
angry
furious
enraged
put out
touchy
heated

? Write an obituary for Antony. Include his 'Roman' and his 'Egyptian' qualities.

? Mark the following statements true or false:

1. Cleopatra sends a message to Antony that she has joined Caesar's side.
2. Scarus is whipped for kissing Cleopatra's hand.
3. Antony asks Scarus to kill him.
4. Antony's forces run away from the battle.
5. Antony tells Cleopatra to trust only Proculeius.
6. Seleucus brings Antony a message that Cleopatra is alive.

Time for a short break before the preparations for the meeting of the two great manipulators, Caesar and Cleopatra.

Act 5 scene 1

Tributes to Antony

◆ Caesar responds to the news of Antony's death.
◆ Caesar receives a message from Cleopatra.
◆ Proculeius is sent to assure Cleopatra of Caesar's good intentions.
◆ Caesar wants to parade Cleopatra in his triumphant procession.

Dercetas enters Caesar's camp, bearing the sword of Antony. ✪ What is the effect of Antony's sword being presented in this way? What aspects of Antony has the sword symbolized throughout the play? Before he tells Caesar what has happened, Dercetas offers his services to Caesar. He does speak generously of Antony, calling him one who *best was worthy/ Best to be served,* and praises Antony's courage and honour in taking his life with his own hands. ✪ What do you think of Dercetas? Is he a callous opportunist, out for the best deal for himself? Is he just being practical?

Caesar's first words in response to Antony's death are quiet and reflective, expressing the incongruity that such a momentous event has taken place without any public disturbance. Antony's death should have been accompanied by strange events like those which preceded the murder of Julius Caesar, as a mark of its universal importance. At the sight of the sword *stained/ With his most noble blood,* Caesar is moved to tears, saying that the event is enough *To wash the eyes of kings.*

Agrippa and Maecenas pay their tributes to Antony, Agrippa first commenting on the strangeness of the fact that our natural feelings cause us to lament events we persistently pursue. ✪ Do you think it is strange that Caesar laments the death of Antony? Both Maecenas and Agrippa acknowledge Antony's greatness and his faults. Maecenas says: *His taints and honours/ Waged equal with him,* and Agrippa adds that the gods give us faults to make us human. ✪ Does the objective nature of these tributes make them insincere? Do you think that Maecenas and Agrippa perceive Antony's true greatness? Maecenas comments that Caesar's tears spring from being confronted with a reflection of what his own fate might have been or might be. ❷ Do you think that Caesar is affected by this thought more than by the thought of Antony himself?

Caesar continues his lament, acknowledging that he sought to destroy Antony in the same way that we lance diseases in our bodies. ❷ Why does Caesar see Antony as a part of himself? Caesar is realistic, and admits that he and Antony could not coexist peacefully anywhere in the whole world. Their stars were irreconcilable, and one of them had to defeat the other. Caesar's speech is tortuous, reflecting his confused and disturbed thoughts as he tries to give public shape and utterance to his thoughts about Antony. He presents a catalogue of Antony's roles – *brother, competitor, mate, friend and companion* – before he is interrupted by the arrival of the Egyptian. ❷ How sincere is Caesar's tribute to Antony?

I want Cleopatra alive

It is typical of Caesar's business-like efficiency that he stops his eulogy of Antony to deal with the new development. Cleopatra says that she is waiting to hear Caesar's instructions. ❷ Why does Cleopatra send this message, when she has already determined to take her life? Caesar sends a message to Cleopatra that his treatment of her will be *honourable* and *kindly*. These words are intended to lull Cleopatra into a false sense of security so that she does not foil Caesar by taking her own life. His real intention, as he makes clear to Proculeius, is to parade Cleopatra through the streets of Rome. ❷ Why does Caesar send Proculeius to guard Cleopatra, then Gallus, then Dolabella?

The scene ends with Caesar preparing his account of his role in the wars. He intends to show how reluctantly he was drawn into the conflict, and how *calm and gentle* he has been. ❷ What do you think of Caesar's assessment of his actions?

Act 5 scene 2

'A pair so famous'

◆ Proculeius assures Cleopatra that Caesar means her well.
◆ Caesar's soldiers seize Cleopatra.
◆ Dolabella tells Cleopatra Caesar's real intentions.
◆ Caesar meets Cleopatra.
◆ Cleopatra provides him with a list of her assets.
◆ Her treasurer Seleucus accuses her of keeping back some of her wealth.
◆ A countryman brings Cleopatra asps hidden in a basket of figs.
◆ Iras dies.
◆ Cleopatra applies the asp to her breast and dies.
◆ Charmian dies.
◆ Caesar gives orders for Cleopatra to be buried beside Antony.

Assessing the situation

Cleopatra is contemplating her desolate state, and musing on the fact that everyone, even Caesar, is subjected to the whims of Fortune. By committing suicide she will free herself from the vagaries of chance and change, and will have no more need for the base earthy food that nourishes all human beings from the lowest to the highest. In the first scene of the play, Antony spoke of rising above *our dungy earth* and finding a higher form of nobility through love. ❂ What is the effect of Cleopatra's use of the same word at this point?

Cleopatra addresses Proculeius with dignity, referring to the fact that she, a queen, is now a beggar, and asking that her son should be allowed to rule Egypt. Proculeius's reply, that Caesar is *so full of grace that it flows over*, is supposed to reassure Cleopatra that Caesar will act magnanimously. ❂ Do you recognize Caesar from the description given here? Cleopatra plays the game. She makes a pretty speech of submission to Caesar, acknowledging his greatness and promising obedience. ❂ Does she mean any of it? Does she know Caesar's true intentions?

Suddenly the guards rush in and seize the queen. ❂ Do you think that Proculeius knew that this was going to happen? Cleopatra tries to stab herself, but Proculeius prevents her. He begs her not to destroy herself, but to give Caesar a chance to demonstrate his generosity. Cleopatra, however, vows that she will kill herself. In an intensely emotional speech, she says that she would rather die in a ditch, rot in the Nile or be hanged in chains on the pyramids than be Caesar's prisoner. ❂ What is the effect of the imagery of flies and maggots? What does it reveal of Cleopatra's state of mind?

A vision of Antony

Dolabella takes over the guard from Proculeius. Cleopatra describes to him her dream of Antony, in which *His face was as the heavens* and the earth in comparison was *The little O*, tiny and insignificant. This is the beginning of Cleopatra's magnificent evocation of Antony's transcendental qualities, a vision created out of her loss and desolation. Antony was a Colossus, standing astride the ocean, while his *reared arm/ Crested the world.* The image presents Antony like a god, dominating the globe. His voice was like the music of the spheres to friends, *But when he meant to quail and shake the orb/ He was as rattling thunder.* Antony's anger was elemental and could make the whole world cower and shake.

In Cleopatra's vision, Antony's superhuman qualities raise him to the status of myth. His generosity was a harvest that increased and grew more abundant as it was reaped, and his greatness stood out even when he was indulging in pleasure-loving activities, just as the dolphin's back rises up in the sea. ❂ What interpretation does the phrase *His delights/ Were dolphin-like* put on Antony's pleasures? Think of phrases from earlier in the play that present Antony's behaviour in a less appealing light. Antony had kings to do his bidding, and could dispose of *realms and islands* as casually as if they were loose change falling from his pocket. ❂ What do you think of this image of Antony? What is the effect of Dolabella's denial that such a man existed? Cleopatra's eulogy completes the process by which Antony, in losing worldly power, gained a spiritual and emotional dimension which made him a creature *past the size of dreaming* (greater than anything that could be imagined). Her words create the myth that has its own emotional truth.

Dolabella's sympathy for Cleopatra leads him to tell her what she does already know, that Caesar will lead her in triumph. ✪ How will this knowledge affect Cleopatra's responses when she meets Caesar?

Face to face

Cleopatra and Caesar play a game of verbal fencing. Cleopatra calls him master and lord, and kneels before him, confessing her weakness. ✪ Does Cleopatra really think that she suffers from female frailties? Is Caesar likely to believe her? Caesar claims that he will regard the harms Cleopatra has inflicted on him as done by chance, and that he will excuse Cleopatra's faults. His words convey a threat and a warning not to contemplate suicide. If Cleopatra co-operates, he says, she will benefit from her change in fortunes, but if not, not only will she be deprived of the good things Caesar intends, but her children will be destroyed.

Cleopatra is enraged when Seleucus refuses to agree that she has declared all her wealth, and hurls abuse at him: *Slave, soulless villain, dog!* ✪ Why does he humiliate Cleopatra in this way? Cleopatra's servants have always been loyal to her. Does Seleucus see an opportunity of impressing Caesar here? It is not clear why Cleopatra kept some of her assets in reserve. After all, if she is intending to kill herself she will have no need of money. It might indicate that she is not finally resolved to die. On the other hand, Cleopatra may be working with Seleucus to convince Caesar that she intends to live. Caesar accepts her explanation that she has reserved some items as gifts for his wife Livia, and for Octavia, to encourage them to intercede for her. ✪ How likely is this? How do you interpret the incident with Seleucus?

Caesar reassures Cleopatra that he will not claim any of the assets she has listed, and that he regards her with *care and pity*. ✪ Does Caesar think that Cleopatra believes him? Cleopatra has seen through Caesar's words, and her shrewd assessment of his real intentions is confirmed by Dolabella's revelation that Caesar plans for Cleopatra and her children to be sent to Syria to be part of his triumph. It is likely that her whispered instructions to Charmian involve the arrangements for her suicide, and Iras's lyrical *The bright day is done/ And we are for the dark* echoes earlier associations with death as the coming of darkness and the extinguishing of light.

Cleopatra gives a graphic description of how she and Antony and her women will be displayed in Caesar's procession. What Caesar intends will destroy the myth that is Cleopatra and reduce her to a figure of fun and contempt, the subject of ridicule for the vulgar people, ballad makers and comedians. Her greatness and her complexity will be reduced to a crude stereotype. She will finally and unbearably be the centre of a theatrical set-piece over which she has no control and which destroys her royal identity. Instead, she plans to die in a way which will seal her mythical status. She asks her women to fetch her *best attires* so that she may be shown *like a Queen*. The allusion to her first meeting with Antony recalls the stage-managed presentation on the River Cydnus, and reinforces the idea that Cleopatra's death will be a similar piece of contrivance. ❂ What do you think about Cleopatra's arrangements for her death?

A rural fellow

As Cleopatra waits for the countryman, she prepares herself for death by discarding the womanly side of her nature and rejecting the moon as her planet. The moon is fleeting, it waxes and wanes, and Cleopatra now needs to become *marble-constant*. Cleopatra's character has been mercurial, unpredictable, inconsistent; now she must assume the firmness and coldness of marble.

The interlude with the clown brings a new dimension to the focus on death. The tension is heightened through his innuendo and muddled speech. The repetition of *worm* for asp, with its phallic associations, brings an erotic undertone to the conversation, and the humour created by his misuse of words and reluctance to depart is gentle and consoling. ❂ Why is the scene with the clown included? How does it shape your response to Cleopatra's death?

The death of Cleopatra

Charmian and Iras help to prepare Cleopatra for death, dressing her in her crown and robes so that she will die as the Queen of Egypt. The nobility of her appearance is matched by her words: *I have/ Immortal longings in me.* Cleopatra musters her courage by calling on the spirit of Antony to praise her noble act, and by reminding herself that she is outwitting Caesar. She calls Antony *husband*, a Roman concept, and one which her courage in performing this Roman act of suicide gives her the right to claim. Antony had died as a *bridegroom*, and Cleopatra will die as his bride. She is transformed into *fire and air*; now she contains no trace of the baser elements of earth and water.

Cleopatra's words create her own transcendence, raising her above and beyond earthly limits. At the same time we are reminded of her common humanity, as she applies the asp to her breast and calls it the baby that sucks the nurse asleep. This image of ordinary womanhood with its daring transposition of death and life brings tenderness to Cleopatra's majesty, just as her greatness is enhanced by Charmian's description of her as *A lass unparalleled.* ❂ How do you respond to the element of self-consciousness in Cleopatra's death? What do you think of its theatrical nature?

Charmian's and Iras's final ministrations to their mistress are a moving tribute to her humanity and her majesty. Iras dies before Cleopatra, and Charmian's last act before applying the asp to herself is to close Cleopatra's eyes and adjust her crown. ❂ What prediction is fulfilled at this point? Charmian's final words affirm Cleopatra's royalty: *a princess/ Descended of so many royal kings.*

At the same time, the scene contains elements which might be thought to undermine the sense of majesty. Iras's death spurs on Cleopatra to follow her example in case Iras is the one to receive Antony's kiss. ❂ What do you think of this spurt of jealousy? The crooked crown that Charmian has to straighten mars the appearance of perfection to which Cleopatra aspires. ❂ To what extent do you think that there is a gap between Cleopatra's dramatic self-presentation and the audience's experience of her? Is the atmosphere of ritual and ceremony at all flawed?

With wonderful timing, Cleopatra has outwitted Caesar. He arrives too late to prevent her death, in truth an *Ass,/ Unpolicied*. He pays tribute to Cleopatra's perfect, unmarked appearance in death, capable of capturing *another Antony/ In her strong toil of grace*. The dialogue between Caesar, the guards and Dolabella consists of deductions and clues about how Cleopatra died. ❂ What is the effect of this?

Caesar orders that Cleopatra should be buried by Antony's side. He pays tribute to the couple's greatness, declaring that *No grave upon the earth shall clip in it/ A pair so famous*. His final words twist the attention to himself, however, when he refers to *his glory which/ Brought them to be lamented*. It is possible that Caesar is referring to Antony here. ❂ Which interpretation do you prefer?

Caesar's speech ends on a typically ambiguous note. He ends the play as the victor, the supreme ruler who is about to usher in the time of universal peace. Caesar is the political and military conqueror. ❂ In what sense may Antony and Cleopatra also be called victors? How might they be considered superior to Caesar? What is your final judgement of them?

Pull it all together

? Write an obituary for Cleopatra.
? What comedy have you found in the play? Make a Mind Map of your ideas.
? What do you agree or disagree with in these statements about the play?

It's about a has-been soldier and a self-obsessed whore who throw away a kingdom for lust.
It celebrates the triumph of the spirit over worldly values.
Its real concerns are power and politics rather than love.
A more accurate title for it would be *Antony and Caesar*.
It should be called *Cleopatra*.

? If you were directing a production of *Antony and Cleopatra*, what reading of it would you present? Which aspects of the play would you emphasize? Make notes or a Mind Map of how you would explain your ideas to your cast. Compare your ideas with a friend's.

? Put the illustrated items in the order in which they appear in the play. Write a caption explaining the significance of each.

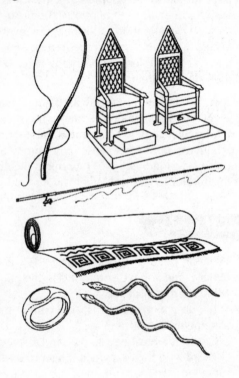

Answers to Commentary tests

OVER TO YOU (P.43)
Antony; Antony; Caesar; Charmian

PULL IT ALL TOGETHER (P.55)
Antony; Menas; Antony; servant; Lepidus

YOUR TURN (P.62)
d; b; c; a
Octavia; Lepidus; Antony; messenger; Octavia

MORE FOR YOU (P.87)
1. false 2. false 3. false 4. false 5. true 6. false

PUTTING IT ALL TOGETHER (P.95)
Items: fishing rod; rolled-up mattress; wedding ring; thrones; whip; asp

Antony and Cleopatra has attracted much critical attention over the centuries. The play is rich in ambiguity, striking poetic imagery and heroic action – all features which have been analysed with different emphases at different times. Early criticism tends to focus on the play's language, characters and structure, while comment from the late twentieth century onwards dwells more on issues of politics and gender.

On *the stage*

Shakespeare's play does not seem to have been staged much after its first performance. One reason for this may be that after the Restoration in 1660 there was a revived interest in neoclassicism, a movement which observed the classical unities of time, place and action, in the face of which *Antony and Cleopatra* seemed sprawling and unstructured. In contrast, John Dryden's play about Antony and Cleopatra, *All for Love or The World Well Lost* (1677), was popular well into the nineteenth century. ✪ What does Dryden's title suggest about his interpretation of the story? This play does observe the classical unities, being set entirely during the last day of the lives of Antony and Cleopatra, and was so popular that passages from it were inserted into Shakespeare's original drama when it eventually found its way back on to the stage in the early nineteenth century.

Shakespeare's own play was revived in 1789 by the famous actor-manager David Garrick. In this revival most of the political scenes were cut and others rearranged, changes in location were restricted, and the language was cleaned up. During the nineteenth century a realistic style of play production was favoured, with carefully researched sets and costumes providing a lifelike representation and feeding the audience's delight in spectacle and visual splendour. ✪ What difficulties would this style present for a production of *Antony and Cleopatra*?

In 1930 in his *Prefaces to Shakespeare*, Harley Granville-Barker praises the play's theatrical techniques and brings attention to the staging possibilities of *Antony and Cleopatra*. His essay illuminates the effects of the shifts of scene, and shows how the story is moulded in the development of character.

Throughout the twentieth century, *Antony and Cleopatra* has been a popular choice for the Royal Shakespeare Company and the National Theatre, as well as many smaller companies. The modern tendency is to perform the complete version of the play. Some productions make use of technology and theatrical effects, for example to stage visual representations of the imagery and of the Roman Empire. ✪ What particular interests do you think the play holds for a modern audience? What do you think are the main challenges facing an actor playing Cleopatra?

Early Romantic criticism

In the early nineteenth century, with the waning of the application of strict classical criteria, *Antony and Cleopatra* attracted a lot of favourable comment. The poet Coleridge praised the play's poetry, and wondered if it was a good enough work to rank alongside the four great tragedies *Hamlet*, *Othello*, *King Lear* and *Macbeth*. ✪ Do you think that *Antony and Cleopatra* is a tragedy? Coleridge was impressed with the profound art displayed in the character of Cleopatra, admiring the depth and energy of her passion even though it springs from a deeply licentious nature and depends on various stimuli. William Hazlitt, in *The Characters of Shakespeare's Plays* (1817), was also fascinated by the presentation of Cleopatra, which he called a masterpiece. Hazlitt described her fascinating allure, claiming that although she has great and inexcusable faults, her death almost redeems them. Hazlitt admired the way that Cleopatra keeps her queen-like status to the end.

Interest in character

The nineteenth-century focus on character is perhaps most famously presented by A. C. Bradley, the influential critic whose *Oxford Lectures in Poetry* (1909) contains an illuminating consideration of the play's unique qualities.

Bradley has several criticisms of *Antony and Cleopatra*, such as its lack of dramatic narrative, the fact that Antony does not display the tragic hero's inner struggle, and its failure to inspire pity and terror to the same degree as the other Shakespearian tragedies. In fact, Bradley finds little of a tragic nature in the first half of the play. Bradley considers that the play is not a great tragedy, but his discussion of the political irony and supernatural elements and his analysis of the characters of Antony and Cleopatra are perceptive and thought-provoking.

Focus on language and imagery

As we move further into the twentieth century, interest in character is replaced by emphasis on the play's poetic structure and themes. In *The Imperial Theme* (1931), G. Wilson Knight focuses on the transcendental nature of the love between Antony and Cleopatra as expressed through the life of the poetry. His reading of the play discounts the human and narrative elements and considerations of praise and blame. Instead Wilson Knight interprets the play as a celebration of the power of ennobling love, and discusses how the imagery of magnificence and ascent creates the play's soaring vision and vindication of spiritual values.

Recent approaches

From the second half of the twentieth century, criticism has focused more on the ambiguities of the play and the limitations of attempting a single unified reading. Interest consists less in drawing out the meaning of a text than in considering the conditions and contexts in which texts are written and meaning is made. In *The Common Liar* (1973), Janet Adelman moves criticism in this direction in a discussion that challenges certainties of judgement. She engages with the play's uncertainties and suggests that it does present us with difficulties in judgement, drawing us in to the structures created by the language and at the same time offering a contradiction of them. Adelman's interest in the poetry is not in its magnificence but in the way the poetic language makes claims that we can neither believe nor wholly disbelieve.

Historical context

H. Neville Davies (*Jacobean Antony and Cleopatra*, 1985) discusses *Antony and Cleopatra* in the context of Jacobean court politics. He sees a parallel between James I and Octavius Caesar. Octavius (Augustus) Caesar established the 'Pax Romana', a period of peace. James was England's version of Augustus, an imperial peacemaker who maintained order in a united kingdom. His coronation medal showed James wearing a laurel wreath, and a Latin inscription named him Caesar Augustus of Britain. ✪ Is the play supportive of this Jacobean propaganda? Is the portrayal of Caesar in *Antony and Cleopatra* a veiled criticism of James I? The answer lies in how you interpret the play's depiction of Octavius Caesar. ✪ Could he be presented in a flattering or appealing light, in some places at least?

Cultural materialism

Jonathan Dollimore's *Radical Tragedy* (1989) argues that Shakespeare's tragedies mediate the changes that were occurring in the society of the time. The methodology Dollimore employs, which involves examining cultural formations, is known as cultural materialism. In *Antony and Cleopatra* he suggests that the clash between Antony and Octavius represents the differences between types of power, the old-fashioned heroism and honour displayed by Antony and the new practical-hard-headed civil power represented by Caesar. Dollimore offers an alternative to a Romantic reading of the play, seeing the relationship of Antony and Cleopatra as having its basis in power, their personal conflicts reflecting the broader scope of the political arena.

Gender issues

Linda Fitz's essay *Egyptian Queens and Male Reviewers: Sexist Attitudes in Antony and Cleopatra Criticism* (1977) is a ground-breaking attempt to move discussion of *Antony and Cleopatra* towards a consideration of Cleopatra as a tragic protagonist, a view which presents a challenge to male-centred literary criticism. The traditional assumption is that tragedy is masculine, and that Antony embodies tragic values. Cleopatra, on the other hand, has been seen as a threat by male critics, who fear her aggressive and manipulative behaviour and see her as a representative of the worst aspects of women. Fitz makes a case for demythologizing Cleopatra and viewing her as a complex being, not as the embodiment of exotic inscrutability. Cleopatra should be assessed more fairly without the sexist distortion which has dominated previous discussion.

Kate Flint's essay *Significant Otherness: sex, silence and Cleopatra* (1990) takes a further look at representations of Cleopatra, and considers the play in relation to current sexual and international politics. Flint points out that in the nineteenth century Cleopatra was seen as a dangerous contradiction to the ideal of womanhood, representing what Victorian men most disliked and distrusted. At the same time, her orientalism provided an opportunity for some voyeuristic, vicarious enjoyment of female sexuality. In the twentieth century, Flint says, the gap between East and West is not as significant as political differences such as those between democracy and authoritarianism. ✪ How might political changes in the world (for example, those in Eastern Europe) affect future interpretations of the play?

Colonization

Representations of and responses to Cleopatra have been complicated by her association with the Orient and by the Western fascination with the East. Edward Said's *Orientalism* (1978) shows that Western attitudes have constructed the Orient along certain lines, turning it into a kind of exotic theatre in which Cleopatra is one of many images which evoke its strange, rich world. Said's theory presents another way of looking at the play: not only is Cleopatra made an erotic figure through male-dominated perceptions, but she is also a focal point for an examination of the Roman attitude to colonization. Said shows that Cleopatra and Egypt have been reduced to stereotypes and clichés, and that the representation of Cleopatra as unfamiliar and exotic is a Western construction which is credible only from a Western perspective. Cleopatra defends her country against Roman imperialism, and the play shows us the political interaction between the Roman drive to annex and colonize, and the Egyptian response to its imperial offensive.

In *all your study, in coursework, and in exams, be aware of the following:*

- **Characterization** – the characters and how we know about them (e.g. speech, actions, author description), their relationships, and how they develop.
- **Plot and structure** – story and how it is organized into parts or episodes.
- **Setting and atmosphere** – the changing physical scene and how it reflects the story (e.g. a storm reflecting chaos).
- **Style and language** – the author's choice of words, and literary devices such as imagery, and how these reflect the **mood**.
- **Viewpoint** – how the story is told (e.g. through an imaginary narrator, or in the third person but through the eyes of one character – 'She was furious – how dare he!').
- **Social and historical context** – the author's influences (see 'Context').
- **Critical approaches** – different ways in which the text has been, or could be, interpreted.

D*evelop your ability to:*

- Relate **detail** to **broader content, meaning and style**.
- Show understanding of the author's **intentions, technique and meaning** (brief and appropriate comparisons with other works by the same author will gain marks).
- Give **personal response and interpretation**, backed up by **examples** and short **quotations**.
- **Evaluate** the author's achievement (how far does she/he succeed – give reasons).

M*ake sure you:*

- Use **paragraphs** and **sentences** correctly.
- Write in an appropriate **register** – formal but not stilted.
- Use short, appropriate quotations as **evidence** of your understanding.
- Use **literary terms** correctly to explain how an author achieves effects.

THE EXAM ESSAY

Planning

You will probably have about 45 minutes for one essay. It is worth spending 5–10 minutes planning it. An excellent way to do this is in the three stages below.

1. **Mind Map** your ideas, without worrying about their order yet.
2. **Order** the relevant ideas (the ones that really relate to the question) by numbering them in the order in which you will write the essay.
3. **Gather** your evidence and short quotes.

You could remember this as the **MOG** technique.

Writing and checking

Then write the essay, allowing five minutes at the end for checking relevance, spelling, grammar and punctuation.

Remember!

Stick to the question and always **back up** your points with evidence in the form of examples and short quotations. Note: you can use '…' for unimportant words missed out in a quotation.

Model answer and plan

The next section consists of an answer to an exam question on *Antony and Cleopatra*, with the Mind Map and plan used to write it. Don't be put off if you think you couldn't write an essay like this yet. You'll develop your skills if you work at them. Even if you're reading this the night before the exam, you can easily memorize the MOG technique in order to do your personal best.

The model answer and plan are good examples to follow, but don't learn them by heart. It's better to pay close attention to the wording of the question you choose to answer, and allow Mind Mapping to help you think creatively and structurally. Before reading them, you might like to do plans of your own to compare with the examples. The numbered comments show why they are good answers.

QUESTION

'Shakespeare gives Cleopatra everything of which he is capable except his final and absolute approval.' (John Danby)

How far do you agree with this assessment of the way Cleopatra is presented?

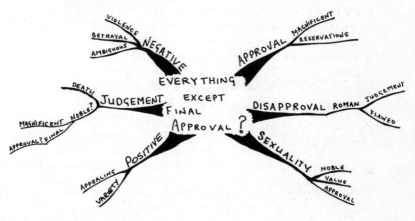

PLAN

◆ address quotation
◆ how disapproval is presented – derogatory images of sexual character
◆ challenge to disapproval – sexuality seen as noble
◆ appealing characteristics
◆ unappealing behaviour
◆ final judgement – her death
◆ ambiguity – perfection marred – total approval withheld

ESSAY

This comment suggests that Cleopatra is a magnificent creation with great appeal for the audience, but that Shakespeare withholds complete approval from the character. In the end, the comment seems to imply, we have reservations about Cleopatra and are left with an impression of a flawed character.[1]

105

Throughout the play, the character of Cleopatra is open to different interpretations. She is presented in such a way that we are constantly aware of the contradictions and paradoxes in her construction, so that our judgement is always challenged. To agree with the Roman view of Cleopatra would certainly be to disapprove of her. She is described as a strumpet and a gypsy who has caused Antony to neglect his Roman duty; she is a 'whore' for whom Antony has given up a kingdom, she is the infamous courtesan who 'made great Caesar lay his sword to bed'; she is the 'ribrauded nag of Egypt'.[2] However, this derogatory presentation of Cleopatra's sexuality, with its attempt to diminish her importance, is balanced and challenged by the value that she and Antony place on their love. Cleopatra is the means through which Antony finds 'the nobleness of life', and lyrical expressions of emotion such as 'Eternity was in our lips and eyes/ Bliss in our brows' bent' present her relationship with Antony as life-enhancing. The poetic intensity of Cleopatra's response to Antony's death, as in 'The crown o'th'earth doth melt', and in her vision of Antony 'whose legs bestrid the ocean' and whose 'voice was propertied/ As all the tuned spheres', has a far greater emotional impact than the Roman interpretations of her expressions of love. In this aspect of Cleopatra at least, I feel that Shakespeare gives Cleopatra absolute approval.[3]

Other aspects of Cleopatra's character are presented in a positive light, inviting our approbation. Cleopatra's fascination lies in her 'infinite variety' and her changes of mood and behaviour. She can be bawdy and earthy, as in her expression of longing for Antony – 'O happy horse, to bear the weight of Antony!' – and in the startling sexuality of her urgent appeal to the messenger: 'Ram thou thy fruitful tidings in mine ears/ That long time have been barren'. Her royalty is stressed throughout the play, and her magnificent self-presentation is captured in Enobarbus's evocation of her meeting with Antony on the Cydnus. What gives the set-piece description added zest and colour is the picture that follows it of Cleopatra out of breath and hopping through the public streets, but making 'defect perfection'. It is part of her peculiar charm 'that the holy priests/ Bless her when she is riggish'. Cleopatra's personality is compelling and multi-faceted.[4]

However, it could be said that much of Cleopatra's behaviour invites disapproval.[5] She is violent towards the innocent messenger; she insists on fighting at Actium then runs away; after Antony's defeat she appears to show public favour to his conqueror's ambassador, and it is possible that she was ready to make terms with Caesar at the end of the play. At the same time, it is possible to find a favourable interpretation for these incidents, or at least to acknowledge their ambiguity.[6]

Whether one agrees that Shakespeare in the end denied Cleopatra absolute approval depends, I think, on how one interprets the end of the play.[7] From Antony's death up to her own suicide, Cleopatra's stature increases as she seems to enter another mode of being: 'now the fleeting moon/ No planet is of mine'. Her awareness of her common humanity is movingly presented as she says that she is now an ordinary woman, ruled by the same emotions as 'the maid that milks/ And does the meanest chares'. In her death, however, she assumes her royal persona, dressing in her crown and robes to meet Antony. Cleopatra encompasses a range of emotion, as she ascends into the higher elements – 'I am fire and air; my other elements/ I give to baser life' – and at the same time evokes the common experience of life and death, asking 'Dost thou not see my baby at my breast/ That sucks the nurse asleep?' The tender ministrations and final deaths of her maids create a moving homage to Cleopatra. Her death is a magnificent ritual through which she triumphs over Caesar and satisfies her 'immortal longings'. Her courageous act earns her the right to call Antony 'husband', and the sexual and spiritual aspects of her nature are combined through the gently bawdy dialogue with the clown and her resolution to perform a 'noble deed'.[8]

Although Cleopatra's death may be seen as a sublime transcending of the paltry world of Caesar, it is surrounded by as much ambiguity as the rest of her life.[9] The period of delay between her resolving to die and her committing the act could be because she wants to die in a non-disfiguring and painless way. For the reputation of Antony and herself, for their mythic status, she wants to appear in death as the legendary beautiful queen who entranced world leaders. At the same time, it could be argued that she holds out for as long as possible because she is hoping to receive favourable terms from Caesar. Her resolve to take her life is strengthened when she knows that Caesar will display her in triumph.

Because of these considerations, I do agree to a large extent with Danby's statement.[10] Cleopatra does not achieve perfection in death because of the doubts and ambiguities that surround both her death and her life. Charmian's final act for her mistress – 'Your crown's awry; I'll mend it' – could indicate something essentially flawed in Cleopatra. She reaches for perfection in death, but does not quite achieve it. In the end, she does not receive the total approval of her creator.

WHAT EARNED THE MARKS?

1 Focus on question.
2 Structured argument.
3 Informed opinion.
4 Confident and accurate style.
5 Argument maintained.
6 Aware of different interpretations.
7 Knowledge and understanding of text.
8 Text confidently used to support argument.
9 Analysis of opposing views maintained.
10 Convincing assessment of opposing views.

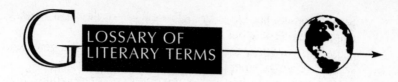

alliteration   the repetition, for effect, of consonant sounds.

allusion   the use of literary, cultural and historical references.

antithesis   combining contrasting ideas or images for dramatic effect.

assonance   the repetition, for effect, of vowel sounds.

classical allusions   referring to characters or events in ancient Greek and Roman literature.

conceit   a fanciful, far-fetched comparison, sometimes sustained at length.

context   the background of social, historical and literary influences on a work.

dialect   regional form of language varying from the standard in vocabulary and grammar.

diction   choice and arrangement of words.

didactic   intended to instruct; in literary criticism, often used in negative sense.

discursive   presenting a logical argument, step by step.

dramatic irony   when a play's audience knows something of which the characters on stage are ignorant.

elision   the suppression of a vowel or syllable.

enjambment   continuation of the sense of a line without pause onto the next line.

epistolary novel   genre of fiction in which the plot unfolds through letters.

exposition   the laying out of the situation from which the plot develops. It can be direct, with a chorus or figure not involved in the action explaining the background, or indirect, as in *Hamlet*, where the situation is revealed in conversations between characters.

feminist criticism   critical approach developed in the 1960s, based on assessing the role of gender in texts. A particular issue is the subordination of women in a patriarchal society.

genre   type of literary work conforming to certain expectations, e.g. tragedy.

groundlings   members of the Elizabethan and Jacobean theatre audience who stood in the pit or floor area in front of the stage. (Also known as 'stinkards'!)

hyperbole   an extravagant, exaggerated figure of speech.

iambic   two-syllable 'foot' or unit of poetry, consisting of an unstressed syllable followed by a stressed one. (See also **pentameter**.)

idiom   a characteristic expression of a language or **dialect**.

image   a word picture bringing an idea to life by appealing to the senses.

industrial novel   novel dealing with the issues of the Industrial Revolution, often set in the north of England, e.g. *North and South* by Elizabeth Gaskell.

irony   a style of writing in which one thing is said and another is meant, used for a variety of effects, such as criticism or ridicule.

Latinate   stemming from Latin.

magical realism   a fiction style which combines mythical elements, bizarre events and a strong sense of cultural tradition, e.g. *Midnight's Children* by Salman Rushdie.

Marxist criticism   critical approach which sees literature in relation to class struggle, and assesses the way texts present social realities.

melodrama   style of drama that appeals to sentiments and passions, usually lacking subtlety.

metaphor   a compressed **simile** describing something as if it were something else, e.g. 'The noble ruin of her magic'.

narrator   in a novel, a character who tells the story. An *omniscient* narrator has complete knowledge of everything that takes place in the narrative.

onomatopoeia   use of words whose sound imitates the thing they describe.

oxymoron   a figure of speech which combines contradictory terms, e.g. 'Royal wench'.

paradox   an apparently contradictory statement containing some truth, e.g. 'whose wind did seem/ To glow the delicate cheeks which they did cool,/ And what they undid did.'

parody an exaggerated copy (especially of a writer's style) made for humorous effect.

pastiche an imitation of another style (of writing), often exaggerated.

pentameter line of poetry consisting of ten syllables. The iambic pentameter (see **iambic**) is the standard line of poetry used by Shakespeare in his plays.

persona an assumed identity.

personification an **image** speaking of something abstract, such as love, death or sleep, as if it were a person or a god.

plot the story; the events that take place and how they are arranged.

polemical (of style) making an argument.

rhetorical expressed with a view to persuade (often used in negative sense).

satire literature which humorously exposes and ridicules vice and folly.

simile an image comparing two things similar in some way but different in others, normally using 'like' or 'as', e.g. 'like a doting mallard'.

standard English the particular form of English, originally based on East Midlands dialect, most often used by educated speakers in formal situations.

stream of consciousness technique exploring the thought processes and unconscious minds of characters; used by writers such as Virginia Woolf and James Joyce.

Structuralism school of critical thought which sees all texts as codes of language.

structure the organization of a text, e.g. narrative, plot, repeated images and symbols.

subplot subsidiary plot coinciding with the main plot and often reflecting aspects of it.

tone the mood created by a writer's choice and organization of words, e.g. persuasive.

viewpoint the way a narrator approaches the material and the audience.

Page references in bold denote major character or theme sections

BUZAN TRAINING COURSES

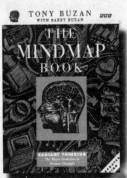

For further information on books, video and audio tapes,
support materials and courses, please send for
our brochure.

Buzan Centres Ltd, 54 Parkstone Road, Poole, Dorset BH15 2PX
Tel: 44 (0) 1202 674676, Fax: 44 (0) 1202 674776
Email: Buzan_Centres_Ltd@compuserve.com

SAINT FRANCIS XAVIER
SIXTH FORM COLLEGE
MALWOOD ROAD, SW12 8EN